A Practical Guide to the Law on Preservation of Common Land and Village Greens

A Practical Guide to the Law on Preservation of Common Land and Village Greens

Rachel Coyle

Barrister, Inner Temple

LLB (Hons), LLM (American Legal Studies-Draper Scholar)

Law Brief Publishing

 Chapter Seven is written by Penny Emmott.

Published 2025 by Law Brief Publishing, an imprint of Law Brief Publishing Ltd
30 The Parks
Minehead
Somerset
TA24 8BT

www.lawbriefpublishing.com

Paperback: 978-1-914608-41-4

To my darling daughters Olivia and Amelia

who keep me busy and focussed.

PREFACE

Sometimes you just need pointing in the right direction. This is the book for you. The basics of what you need to know about Commons and Village Greens:

a. What are they?

b. What are pioneer areas?

c. Can I apply to register it?

d. Can I develop?

This book is designed to bring together the different definitions and understandings.

It is anticipated that the book will serve as a practical guide for landowners, developers, sports clubs, those engaged in offering sports and pastimes and local stakeholders.

The law stated is believe to be accurate and up-to-date as of 1 October 2024.

Rachel Coyle
October 2024

ACKNOWLEDGMENTS

I am grateful to my husband, Ben, for his patience and support while I wrote this book.

I am also grateful to my extended family, my clerks at Exchange Chambers and my instructing clients for their continued support.

I am also grateful to Penny Emmott, co-member of Exchange Chambers, for contributing to this book and writing Chapter Seven.

CONTENTS

CHAPTER ONE

WHAT IS COMMON LAND?

This chapter describes what Common Land is.

A Right of Common

Typically, common land is understood to refer to land over which rights of common are exercised. As was helpfully set out by Winn LJ in *Beckett (Alfred F) Ltd v Lyons [1967] Ch. 449* at [482]:

a. It is a legal right of one or more people;

b. To take or use some part of the natural produce of, or wild animals upon,

c. The land of another.

This is known as Rights of common. They are a type of incorporeal hereditament and nature, profits à pendre.

There can be a profit in common in a range of circumstances:

a. where the owner is entirely excluded from the benefit by the holder/s;

b. where the holder of the profit share in the benefit of the produce with the owner of the soil.

While there are exceptions, if one unlawfully takes or uses said produce, this belongs to the owner of the soil from which it came.

Common Law Definition v Statute Definition

Common Law	**Statute**
Land subject to rights of common. The common land to which the common right attaches is the dominant tenement	Definition stems from the 1965 Act, s22(1) and the Inclosure Act 1845, s.11. S.22(1) states: *"(a) land subject to rights of common (as defined in the Act) whether those rights are exercisable at all times or only during limited periods; (b) waste land of a manor not subject to rights of common",*
A right in common is known as profits à pendre. The grantee takes some part of the land, the products of the land or animal thereon, that belong to another person – see *Beckett (Alfred F) v Lyons [1967] Ch. 449* at 482, per Winn LJ	Reference to the 1965 definition features in other statutes such as the Countryside Act 1968 (open air recreation) and Criminal Justice and Public Order Act 1994 (trespass on common land)
Some part of the benefit in the subject matter (be it hay, grass, animals etc) must remain vested in the owner of the soil – commonality between owner and rights holders.	The 1965 Act definition did not include a town or village green or any land which forms part of a highway. A "town or village green" was separately defined. Oddly, s.22 included "waste land of manor" even though this

was subject to no third-party rights.

Stops when:

i. extinguished;

ii. there is unity of possession;

iii. such rights are released to the owner.

Unhelpfully, s.61(1) of the Commons Act 2006 has no definition at all save that the glossary of terms contained in the Explanatory Notes states that there is no single definition of "common land", "common", or "common rights" due to its complexity. In the case of a sole right in pasture granted to multiple persons and shared between them, i.e stinted pastures, there is no community of use and differs to rights of common. Yet, the 2006 Act seems to suggest this is within the s.61(1) attempted definition.

Must be held for an interest equivalent to a fee simple

Common fields: originate from the manorial system. Occupiers take crops from parts of the field held in severalty, and graze in common when the land is not growing crops. It becomes

commonable after the severalty crop is removed.

Stinted Pastures: sole or several right. No community of use between owner of the soil and the rights holder. The owner has no share.

Different to Easements

Easement	**Rights in Common**
No right to participate in the produce of land of another (often included as a restrictive covenant in leases)	Taking or using some part of the natural produce, or wild animals, upon land of another
Not held in gross – need a dominant tenement	Can be held in gross i.e it does not need to attach to a dominant corporeal hereditament. Be aware of the exceptions in Schedule1 1, but it is now prohibited by s.9 of Schedule 1 of the Commons Act 2006 to sever rights in common which are attached
Not wholly separate to rights in common	Can include easements that are reasonably necessary for the reasonable enjoyment of the principal or primary right – see Buckley LJ in *White v Taylor (No.3) [1969] 1 Ch. 160 at [19].*

Pre 2006, there was the Commons Act 1965. Some rights of common are registered thereunder that have remained unchallenged but which would not satisfy the test in the Commons Act 2006 and subsequent case law to be strictly described as "rights of common."

These days, when mention is made of a "common", this usually means the land itself over which rights of common are exercised.

How do I know from looking at land whether it is a common?

How it looks topologically and geographically is not key. That it is open or enclosed is also not indicative of whether the land is a common or not, despite most commons being unenclosed.

One must focus on the use of the land, which in part depends on location but also on its historic use/s in the past. For instance, is it open grazing land that is in part enclosed that has been made available to farmers, collectively? Is there an unused village green or seemingly random plot of land that at one time was part of manor land which is now being used as a recreation ground for sports such as cricket, pétanque or rugby? Is the land rich in wildlife or steeped in archaeological remains?

Most common land exists as a result of the inclosure movement in the 18th century AD and extinguishment of the manorial system, but not all land used in common with the manorial system is subject to rights of common today.

Commons Act 1965

The 1965 Act was intended to be a definitive statutory registration scheme.

It was designed to provide for public access and management schemes, whereby any ownerless town or village greens would be vested in local authorities, and there be an implied right of access to, and protection for, all greens.

The 1965 Act was enacted to allow for registration of land, rights and ownership up to 2 January 1970.

After that date unregistered land was no longer deemed to be common land and rights of common thereto became unexercisable unless registered.

Objections to any disputed provisional registrations was permitted until July 1972.

The 1965 Act was riddled with difficulties:

a. there were more objections than anticipated;

b. land was registered that should not have been and land was not registered when it should have been;

c. the extent of the land and associated rights had been overstated or understated in some instances;

d. there was no mechanism to enable land registered to be removed once made final.

These are just some of the reasons why the Commons Act 2006 was introduced.

Rachel Coyle is a specialist property barrister who also works in commercial dispute resolution and private client. She acts in all types of commercial and property disputes, whether arising from contract, breach of duty, or otherwise. Rachel's practice also encompasses contentious trusts, wills, and probate (including TOLATA and Inheritance Act claims) and insolvency.

Rachel's expertise in property and commercial law is founded on time spent working in hedging product mis-selling, volunteering in the procurement and commercial team at Stockport Homes, paralegal work at law firms such as DWF LLP and on secondments at Hyde Housing and OneSource. In the USA, she acted pro bono in property and planning matters in the State of Virginia whilst studying for her LLM in American Legal Studies.

Clients that Rachel has worked with include global banks, U.K. solicitors' firms with domestic and/or international clients, a Cypriot law firm, start-ups, private equity sponsors, local government departments and councils, large landowners and property management companies, charities, high net worth individuals and more vulnerable members of society. As part of her private client practice, she assists and represents trustees, beneficiaries and estates with inheritance and administration-related matters

Rachel can assist with advice, negotiation, mediation and litigation to the Court of Appeal level. Rachel has appeared in the High Court in the Business and Property Courts, Companies Court, Queens Bench Division, Chancery Division and Administrative Division. She has built a strong experience in the County Court to multi track level. She also has experience in the First-tier Tribunal (Property Chamber) and First-tier Tribunal (Land Registration) cases including service charges, enfranchisement, boundary disputes, easements, breaches of covenant, adverse possession and the Housing Act 2004.

What was registrable under the 1965 Act?

Those which were registrable under the 1965 Act included:

a. *Wastes:* meaning waste land of a manor. Typically consists of open land with rights of common exercisable by the owners or occupiers of enclosed land. The owner of the soil is entitled to any residue of a product remaining after the rights granted away have been realised. The position under the 2006 Act is that one cannot create a new right other than by express grant providing said right is attached to land, and the land can sustain said right with existing rights. New rights of common cannot be created over existing town or village greens;

b. *Stinted Pastures*: the owner of the soil has no residual interest in the grazing and the land the land is subject to a sole profit. The whole of the grazing has been granted away as a separate incorporeal hereditament, to one or more people, and then divided into equal shares (stints).

c. *Common Fields*: crops are harvested by tenants of the manor (historically) on strips and the land, after harvest, is then opened for communal grazing in "open" season. This is "open fields". Few remain today;

d. *Regulated Pastures*: land is used in common by a number of people with a fixed right to graze a certain number of animals. The graziers own the land in undivided shares, but the grazing is directly related to a share in the land.

Not registrable:

a. Royal Forests;

b. Land exempted by order of a Minister – s.11(1) of the 1965 Act contains a list of exemptions.

The Commons Act 2006, s.22, provides provisions for amendments to be made to the register for registration of common land under the 2006 Act that was unregistered post 1965 Act.

CHAPTER TWO

CLASSIFICATION

This chapter describes what classes there are

Classification of rights of common

Rights of common is a species of profit à prendre that concerns:

a. the *legal nature* of the profit including profits into appendant, appurtenant, in gross and pur cause de vicinage;

b. the *subject matter* of the grant such as profits into pasturage, estovers, pannage, turbary piscary, rights in the soil and rights to animals.

Legal nature of rights of common

Appendant or appurtenant

Most grazing rights were, historically, passed on or sold but only with the farm to which they were attached.

Such rights were to be enjoyed by the occupier for the time being and so could not be separated or "severed" from the farm.

A grazing right for a fixed number, on the other hand, was known as a right "in gross", and unattached to any holding.

In *Bettison v Langton* [2002] 1 A.C. 27 it was held that the 1965 Act placed no restrictions on the common law rule that grazing rights appurtenant to land, if limited to a fixed number of animals, could be severed from the land to which they were attached. This resulted in a conversion to rights in gross.

Pursuant to s.15 of the 1965 Act grazing rights formerly limited by levancy and couchancy became rights to graze for a fixed number of animals and could also be severed. As set out aforesaid, since s.9 of the 2006 Act, severance of most rights of common is prohibited, save that this provision does not affect previously severed rights.

The classes of animals allowed with a common appendant were only those required to plough or manure the land i.e "commonable animals". How many animals that were permitted for such a purpose was dependent on the quantity.

A common appurtenant generally shared the feature with common appendant that it was a right attached to land, being an incorporeal hereditament appurtenant to a corporeal hereditament. A right appurtenant did not arise by privilege of law like common appendant, but by express, implied or presumed grant

Commons in gross

A right in gross only as a right which is not annexed to a hereditament, whether corporeal or incorporeal, and classify all others as appurtenant.

Vicinage

The general nature of this right is described by Blackstone as follows:

> *"Common because of vicinage, or neighbourhood, is where the inhabitants of two townships, which lie contiguous to each other, have usually intercommoned with one another; the beasts of the one straying mutually into the other's fields, without any molestation from either. This is indeed only a permissive right, intended to excuse what in strictness is a trespass in both, and to prevent a multiplicity of suits: and therefore, either township may inclose and bar out the other, though they have intercommoned time out of mind. Neither has any person of one town a right to put his beasts originally into the other's common; but if they escape, and stray thither of themselves, the law winks at the trespass."*

There are a number of conditions required before a common of vicinage may exist, as set out in *Heath v Elliott (1838) 4 Bing.N.C. 388; 132 E.R. 836;*

a. The right is only exercisable from land where there is a lawful right for the animals to be;

b. The land must be contiguous and unenclosed;

c. The quantity of animals turned to the "home" common must not exceed the capacity of that common;

d. There must always be, or at least have been, a mutuality of rights over and between the contiguous commons.

The mutual interest may only be terminated unilaterally by the total enclosure of one of the commons. Partial enclosure will leave the unenclosed portion still subject to common of vicinage but has the effect of terminating the rights over and from the portion.

Helpful guidance is also set out in *Jones v Robin* (1845) 10 Q.B. 581; 116 E.R. 221; (1847) 10 Q.B. 620; 116 E.R. 235 as to *pur cause de vincage* whereby it was stated:

> *"It must be considered to be established that a common … pur cause de vicinage, is not properly a right of common or profit à prendre, but rather an excuse for a trespass…The question then arises … whether it is essential, to support such a claim, that it should be between persons having rights of common properly so called, or at least that there should be commoners on both sides, or whether it may exist between two proprietors whose lands are not subject to common rights … If this had been the only question, we think, after a careful consideration of the arguments and of the authorities, we should probably have held that it might exist between two proprietors without commoners on either side. The reason of the law which sanctions a claim of this sort is either on account of its convenience, it being better to intercommon than that each should watch his own cattle; or to avoid multiplicity of suits … and both these reasons apply to owners who interpasture as well as to commoners, though, as to the latter, not to the same degree … On the whole the authorities appear to shew that there is no necessity for commoners on both sides in order to give validity to a claim for common pur cause de vicinage, though, where such common exists, most frequently there are commoners on both sides."*

Since the Commons Act 2006 Act it is not possible to create rights of common by prescription.

Vicinage arises through proof of a custom on the land, which requires immemorial user. Once a claim to *vicinage* has been established, although the right is limited in character as it is determinable, it is to be classified as a right of common; it cannot be properly viewed as a profit à prendre.

Subject matter of rights of common

The most often encountered are pannage, pasturage, estovers, turbary, piscary, common in the soil, Sole Profits, Sheepwalks and Animals Ferae Nature.

Pannage

Pannage is a more limited right to graze pigs such as in woodlands or forests. The definition is, so far as it is possible to define such an ancient right, set out in *Chilton v Corporation of London* (1878) 7 Ch.D. 562:

> *"They all agree that the right of pannage is simply a right granted to an owner of pigs—the grant was usually to an owner of land of some kind who kept pigs—to go into the wood of the grantor of the right and to allow the pigs to eat the acorns or beech-mast which fell upon the ground. That is what the right has always been defined to be. The pigs have no right to take a single acorn or any beech-mast off the tree, either by themselves or by the hands of those who drive them. There is not even a right to shake the tree. It is only aright to eat what has fallen to the ground."*

Pasturage

The right of pasturage is a right of common of pasture. It is the most often encountered common right.

Pursuant to *Samborne v Harilo* (1621) Bridgman J. 9 at 10, it is the right to take grass by the mouths of cattle. The commoner has no property in the grass until he or she takes it by grazing. This means that until such taking of the same, the commoner has no action in trespass.

Pasturage is not isolated to grass. It includes leaves, nuts and other foliage.

The right does not include a right to cut any herbage. Any collateral rights in respect of the same, however, must be evidenced by an entry on the commons registers, despite the same not being a conclusive limitation or evidence of said right.

With a right of pasturage there is a right to enter the land and it is not unusual to encounter the easements necessary such right to be properly exercised.

Estovers

This tends to relate to fuel or attaches to a house/building. As to the latter, as per *Sir Henry Nevil's Case* (1569) 1 Plow. 377 at 381; 75 E.R. 572 it is annexed to the building. Pursuant to s.9, schedule 1, since the Commons Act 2006 it is not possible to sever the right from the land to which is attached.

There are 4 main types:

(1) *Estoveria adificandi*: fell and take timber-trees to repair/rebuild houses.

(2) *Estoveria ardendi*: to cut and take shrubs, decayed and dead trees etc, to burn.

(3) *Estovaria arandi*: to cut and take timber to repair tenant's equipment that is used for the purposes of getting in hay or corn.

(4) *Estoveria claudendi*: to take either proper timber for use to inclose open fields.

Many commons of estovers were registered under the 1965 Act and so if the cope of it is unknown, those reading ought to consult the register. For example, there might be a limited quantity that can be taken from the land or the exercise of the same is only exercisable over a set period of time.

Turbary

This is the right to take turf or peat for burning as fuel and whilst historically it was be regarded as a form of estover or right in the soil, it has developed into its own being of two kinds:

(1) *turba*: dry out of the body of the ground. This is peat dug for fuel.

(2) *blestia*, pared from the surface

Where the right is annexed to a house or building the same rules apply as they do to Estovers.

If the right is fixed in quantity and is appurtenant to a house. It too cannot be severed.

A right of turbary may extend over the whole or part of a waste depending upon the terms of the express grant. It can also be implied as confirmed in sections 8 and 9 of the Commons Act 2006.

Piscary

This is the right to take fish from a pond, lake, stream or river where the bed of it belongs to another person.

It is capable of registration as a statutory right of common. Where it is an appurtenant right, it is limited to the needs of the household. It is subject to the same rules as estovers and turbary in relation to severance, apportionment and sale of products.

Rights in the soil

The right to take some part of the soil or minerals from the land of another person is a profit à prendre and right of common. It could exist appurtenant to the tenement or in gross. Often it is in gross such as but not limited to commercial value of mineral and other rights.

A profit, and a right of common, may only exist if the product is part of the soil. Whether this includes minerals deposited on it, on the other hand, has been debated. Such examples include the wind blowing Saharan sand onto land in England. So far as any part of the soil may form the subject matter of a profit, a right of common will often be identified. Example cases include *Maxwell v Martin* (1830) 6 Bing. 522; 130 E.R. 1382 in. This concerned sand, marl and clay.

There are other cases, however, wherein the court has assumed that a colliery tip constituted chattels and had not become part of the realty, see *Ryan Industrial Fuels Ltd v Morgan (VO)* (1965) 1W.L.R. 1347.

It is unclear whether right in the soil includes taking stone or claiming to use a quarry.

Where there are appurtenant rights, unless the quantity is fixed by the grant, the amount which may be taken is governed by the needs of the dominant tenement. For instance, a party seeking the benefit of such a right will typically have to show that the property is in disrepair and that the sand, gravel etc will be used to carry out those repairs, see by way of example *Peppin v Shakespear.* If there is surplus, is does not mean that there is a right to sell the same or to convert the right in gross. This is in line with the Agricultural Land (Removal of Surface Soil) Act 1953 wherein it is set out that it is a criminal offence to remove the surface soil from agricultural land and then sell it subject to permissions and the amount.

Sole profits

This is not to be confused with a profit in common because as to sole profits, the owner of the soil over which it is exercised has no residual interest in the product. Examples include agricultural produce of the land, excluding timber, but including swepage. Such examples are known as vesture. As to herbage, this is limited to taking of grass by grazing but is often combined with the right to pasture. It is the latter, typically, when the grass may only be taken through the mouths of cattle. As with the right of vesture the owner of herbage may sue in trespass but may not interfere with the soil.

A sole profit may be held for an interest equivalent to a fee simple or for a term of years and in those circumstances, it was registrable as statutory rights of common under the 1965.

Courts have held that absent a deed suggesting otherwise, the possession of most of the produce in a year carried with it the rebuttable presumption that the owner ship of the land coincided with the right.

Sheepwalks

A sheepwalk means part of a waste where one has customarily grazed a flock of sheep and the sheep have acclimatised.

Settling, and acclimatising, a flock of sheep to a particular part of a waste enables the sheep to become used to the weather conditions and the shepherd knows where to find them. Boundaries in respect of the same are often denoted by being partially fenced, for example.

If there is a change of ownership of the associated land, the settled flock is normally conveyed with the land and not sold separately and the tenant/shepherd may be paid for this.

In Wales a substantial amount of the waste land was vested in the Crown through ownership of manors or as a result of inclosure awards whereas in England, the owner is more often known or the shepherd/tenant has come to treat the land as his or her own in the absence of an absentee owner. This can cause tempers to flare if farmers claim rights of common over the same land. The alternative would be to assert that one of the farmers has an exclusive right of pasturage over the land as appurtenant to his or her farm.

Attempts to describe sheepwalk include *Attorney General v Reveley*. It was explained as being the exercise of a right of common over a waste which by mutual consent or acquiescence was exercisable over that portion of the waste contiguous to, or conveniently depastured with, the enclosed land. It cannot be assumed, therefore, that arrangements in respect of more or less exclusive use is evidence of or will attract a finding of possession of the land being in the commoner.

Animals ferae naturae

The right to take and carry away animals ferae naturae is a profit à prendre and may exist as a right of Common, see by way of example, *Duke of Portland v Hill* (1866) L.R. 2 Eq. 765. This right of common is sometimes confused with sporting rights. As Lord Campbell LC in *Ewart v Graham* (1859) 7 H.L.C. 330 at 334; 11 E.R. 132 said:

> *"The property in animals, ferae naturae, while they are on the soil, belongs to the owner of the soil, and he may grant a right to others to come and take them by a grant of hunting, shooting, fowling and so forth; that right may be granted by the owner of the fee simple, and such a grant is a licence of a profit à prendre."*

A profit to take animals is capable of registration as a right of common if it is held for an interest equivalent to a fee simple and use shared with the owner of the soil. However, it is worth noting by contrast, *Re Lustleigh Cleave, Lustleigh, Devon (No.1)* (1978) 209/D/114–130, wherein it was decided that a right to kill and carry away wild duck was a profit but is different to a right of shooting, even when joined with a right to take game, it was being exercised not for the value of the game as food but for leisure/fun.

CHAPTER THREE

REGISTRATION: THE 1965 ACT

This Chapter explains what the Commons Registration Act 1965 is and why it might still be relevant.

Why are we in a permanent state of transition?

The 1965 Act provided for the registration of all common land and town or village greens, and rights of common exercisable over such land.

Part 1 of the 2006 Act is intended to wholly replace the 1965 Act so as to assist in the maintenance of the register given that there were mistakes and lack of consistency geographically.

The Act has been repealed in its entirety in the pioneer areas in England pursuant to the Commons Act 2006, Sch.6 Pt 1, the Commons Act 2006 (Commencement No.4 and Savings) (England) Order 2008 (SI 2008/ 1960) art.2(1)(h) and the Commons Act 2006 (Commencement No.7, Transitional and Savings Provisions) (England) Order 2014 (SI 2014/3026) art.3(1)(i) (repeals of certain provisions in the 1965 Act have been brought into force with national application in other instruments).

In England, as from 1 October 2006, ss.8, 9 and 13(a) of the 1965 Act have been repealed and as from 6 April 2007, s.13(b) has been repealed. As from 1 December 2010, sections 4 to 7 and sections 17 and 18 have been repealed.

Outside the pioneer areas, therefore, the 1965 Act applies.

The Register

Under the 1965 Act every registration authority must maintain:

a. a register of common land; and

b. a register of town or village greens.

It must include:

a. a general part: The purpose of the general part of the register is to contain particulars of any "straddling" agreement. This may provide that land in the area of one registration authority is to be the responsibility of a neighbouring authority for the purposes of registration under the 1965 Act. It includes the particulars of any land situated in the area of the registration authority to which the registration provisions do not apply as well the of any transfer to or from the registration authority. The form of the general part of the register is prescribed as per General Regulations reg.4(2), Sch.1 Form 1.

b. a map;

c. register units: Each register unit corresponds to the land contained in the original application for provisional registration of that land, or the land registered on the initiative of the registration authority. The land section of each register unit contains a description and particulars of the registered land with reference to the register map. The rights section of each register unit contains the registrations of the rights of common registered as exercisable over the land comprised in the land section of the register unit. *The ownership section* of each register unit contains the registration of every person registered as owner of any part of the land comprised in the register unit.

The Commons Registration (General) Regulations 1966 (SI 1966/1471) applies to how the register is to appear.

Notes are often included in relation to matters affecting the public, charitable interests and private rights and interests.

The public may inspect the register at any reasonable time pursuant to s.3(2) of the 1965 Act. If one would like a copy of the register, it may be obtained if a fee is paid. The fee is fixed by the authority pursuant to regulations 33 and 34 of the General Regulations, Schedule 3.

Registration requirements

Pursuant to section 4, between 2 January 1967 and 31 July 1970 there was a mandatory registration period for all common land and town or village greens.

This meant that any land capable of being registered, and remaining unregistered after 31 July 1970, was deemed no longer to be common land, or a town, or village green, and no rights.

All applications were to be made within one of two consecutive application periods and in any event by 2 January 1970.

Registration of waste land of a manor or town or village green without application, and after the closing date for applications, was additionally possible between 3 January 1970 and 31 July 1970 but it would be provisionally added to the register where no application had been made for that purpose during either of the application periods.

Where a right came to be provisionally registered over any land which had not itself already been registered, the registration authority was also to register that land as common land.

Two notices were required. The registration advertised when there was a provisional registration twice. On the second occasion, it had to be in a prescribed form.

Written evidence was not required but if an objection was anticipated, it was advisable. Some landowners, however, were not aware that their land had been registered until it was too late to make an objection but the provisional registration became final regardless.

Sometimes the registration authority received at two or more applications to register the same parcel of land. Where this occurred, the land identified in the first application to be received was provisionally registered in the requisite manner. All further applications for the registration of the same parcel of land were then noted in the land section of the register. Further conflicts arose where the same parcel of land was provisionally registered both as common and town or village green.

Objections

Where an objection was made, the objector and applicant were encouraged to negotiate. Section 5(6) of 1965 Act provided that where an objection was made to a registration then, unless the objection was withdrawn or the registration cancelled before the end of such period as might be prescribed, the registration authority was required to refer the matter to a Commons Commissioner for resolution.

The "late objection" procedure could only be utilised in certain limited circumstances, such as:

(a) Where an objection had been properly made but which had still not been determined by a Commons Commissioner

(b) Where there was a conflicting registration;

(c) Where there was a conflicting registration of land which had been registered as part of a common land registration and also as a part of a village green registration (a double registration).

This objection procedure was not available after the relevant land was registered and this was final.

Commissioners

The Court of Appeal confirmed the remit of the commissioners' powers in *Re West Anstey Common* [1985] Ch. 329 CA. In that case a parcel of land, owned or claimed by several owners, provisionally was registered as common land. The decision concerned an objection to only part of the land comprised in the land registration. Sade LJ reviewed the cases and concluded that:

> *"The provisions of s.5(6) [of the 1965 Act] which envisage a 'matter' being referred to the commissioner and those of s.6(1) which envisage him 'inquiring into it' presuppose that he must address his mind to a question. That question is, I think, what is to be done about the registration to which objection has been taken? That is the matter which is referred to him."* [1985] Ch. 329 at 340.

This raised the question of what is the status of all the land and all the rights? It was stated that an objection to registration of the land fell to be treated as an objection to registration of any rights over the land. Hence the matter referred to a Commissioner would comprise the validity or otherwise of the whole registration which had been put in question by the objection.

Where a registration of rights required confirmation, the burden was on the Applicant.

Any land capable of being registered before 31 July 1970 and was not, was deemed no longer to be common land, town or village green pursuant to s.1(2) of the 1965 Act. This did not mean that it could not be registered after that date. It could be pursuant to section of the 1965 Act.

Rights of common were not capable of being exercised after that date in relation to such land that was capable of and was not registered.

Greens can be subject to rights of common and itself be regarded as common land.

An application to register a right of common was to be taken as an application also to register the land over which the right was exercisable.

The registration authority had limited authority; ensuring that an application for provisional registration was made. If it was, it was obliged to give effect to the registration, even if it seemed non-sensical.

The 1965 Act provided that any person unhappy with the decision of a Commons Commissioner could appeal by way of case stated to the High Court, but only on a point of law. The appeal was assigned to the Chancery Division.

The actions and decisions of a Commons Commissioner were subject to judicial review by the court. In *R. v Commons Commissioner Ex p. Bostock* [1982] 1 W.L.R. 647 it was confirmed that the usual method of challenging a Commons Commissioner was by way of case stated to the Chancery Division. If the Commissioner exceeded his or her jurisdiction or failed to exercise it, then this would be an application for judicial review. In *Re Sutton Common, Wimborne* [1982] 1 W.L.R. 647 the High Court stated that "the matter" referred to a Commissioner was not the particular dispute which occasioned the reference but, rather, the validity or otherwise of the whole land registration. The owner of the land applied for relief by way of judicial review. It was held that as a matter of law it was necessary to require clear proof of the land registration from the applicants; the Commissioner had failed to exercise his jurisdiction.

The registers under the 1965 Act are conclusive as to the attachment of a right of common to land, where the right is so registered, and that the ownership of that right may be derived from the determination of the ownership of that land in the usual way. However, if registration has *"become final and the court is satisfied that any person was induced by fraud to withdraw an objection to the registration or to refrain from making such an objection; … and … the court deems it just to rectify the register"* (s.14(a) of the 1965 Act) then the High Court can intervene.

Courts are hesitant to intervene, as *McLaren v Kubiak* [2007] EWHC 1065 (Ch) confirms. The High Court struck out the claimant's application for a declaration that a plot of land owned by him was not registrable as a new town or village green for the purposes of s.13 of the 1965 Act on the grounds that this was capable of being decided by the Commissioner and relevant registration authority.

What was registrable?

Common land was defined in section 22(1):

> *"In this Act, unless the context otherwise requires,— 'common land' means—*
>
> *(a) land subject to rights of common (as defined in [the 1965] Act) whether those rights are exercisable at all times or only during limited periods;*
>
> *(b) waste land of a manor not subject to rights of common but does not include a town or village green or any land which forms part of a highway".*

Some examples include:

a. Waste land, whether subject to rights of common at all times or for limited periods, was included as well as common fields which were subject to rights of common;

b. As to land held in undivided shares, the position was that it was not registrable. However, the courts have sought to clarify the position such as in the case of *Re Longton Out Marsh, Lancashire* (1974) 20/U/81 wherein it was stated that "*each cattlegate owner has a right of common over the entirety, not merely over the undivided share of which he is owner;*"

c. As to charitable shares, the definition of land and rights in the 1965 Act also was considered to be insufficient because there are no persons exercising rights over the land of another person. The rights which are exercised are those of beneficiaries under a trust. Failure to register land held on such trust does not mean that the trustee has failed the beneficiaries;

d. Sole vesture, herbage and pasture is expressly included in the definition of rights of common.

Exemptions

Some land is exempted from registration such as the Forest of Dean or because no rights of common had been exercised over the land for at least 30 years (see s.11 of the 1965 Act). There might be local Acts that apply, such as to the Epping Forest which is also exempt.

What was the procedure for registration

Pursuant to s.168 of the 1965 Act, an application to register a right of common was to be taken as an application also to register the land over which the right was exercisable.

Where the right was attached to land, the registration authority was required to register the right by recording details of the land to which the right was attached. The land to which a right of common is attached is a part of a right of common: it is the owner of that land (the dominant tenement) who is entitled to exercise the right. Pursuant to s.18(3) of the Commons Act 2006, the register becomes conclusive evidence of the attachment of a right to land.

An application could be made on one of four forms:

(a) Application for the registration of land as common land (Form 7);

(b) Application for the registration of land as a town or village green (Form 8);

(c) Application for the registration of a right of common (Form 9);

(d) Application for the registration of a claim to ownership of land (Form 10).

New common land and Non-Registration

Pursuant to s.1(2) of the 1965 Act:

> *"After the end of such period, not being less than three years from the commencement of this Act, as the Minister may by order determine [31 July 1970]269—*
>
> *(a) no land capable of being registered under this Act shall be deemed to be common land or a town or village green unless it is so registered; and*
>
> *(b) no rights of common shall be exercisable over any such land unless they are registered either under this Act or [in the register of title]."*

The effect of this is that rights remaining unregistered were extinguished as they ceased to be exercisable. As was said in *Oxfordshire CC v Oxford City Council* [2006] 2 A.C. 674

> *"that the effect of non-registration was to extinguish such rights of recreation as may have existed by custom or statutory allotment and were registrable on the appointed day".*

A provisional registration of land or rights, in itself, conferred no status on the land, nor did it protect the rights. Section 10 of the 1965 Act conferred conclusiveness on certain matters registered, but not where the registration remained provisional. Thus, for example, if rights of common were provisionally registered, the applicant for registration could not just point to the entry on the register to obtain an injunction to activity on the land; they need evidence of the existence of the rights.

Section 7 of the 1965 Act provided that where no objection to registration was made, or if all objections were withdrawn at the end of the objection period the registration should become final. The Court of Appeal confirmed in *Corpus Christi College (Oxford) v Gloucestershire CC* [1983] Q.B. 360 has held that even where land had clearly been wrongly registered as common land, save if there is the commission fraud as set out above, the 1965 Act did not enable such land to be removed from the register once the registration had become final.

More recently, the conclusiveness of registration was considered in *R (on the application of Littlejohns) v Devon CC* 6 [2016] EWCA Civ 446 when the Court of Appeal recognised that the question it had to answer was this: was it possible to acquire a right of common by virtue of an express grant or (as in the present case) user after 2 January 1970 over land registered under the Commons Registration Act 1965 on or before 31 July 1970. The right claimed was for 224 "livestock units". It was stated that the right to graze those animals was attached to Minehouse Farm and Estrayer Park which were owned by the Littlejohns. The National Farmers' Union, on behalf of the Littlejohns, sent a formal notice of intention to register within the relevant time period but it was never formally registered. On 28 May 2014 the county council then refused the Littlejohns' application. The reason given was that, although they had provided evidence that rights of common had been exercised by the owners of the farms over the register units for more than 30 years, the Council was of the view that a right of common could not be created by prescription after 2 January 1970 over land that had been registered as common land under the 1965 Act. The Court of Appeal decided that the extinguishment of rights of common effected by the 1965 Act only applies to rights exercisable over land registered under the 1965 Act.

Section 13

Section 13(b) of the 1965 Act provided for regulations to be made to enable the registers to be amended where *"any land becomes common land or a town or village green"*. Section 13(b) has been repealed in relation to the non-pioneer areas. The regulations giving effect to s.13(b) are the Commons Registration (New Land) Regulations 1969. New Land Regulation 3:

> *"(1) Where, after 2 January 1970, any land becomes common land or a town or village green, application may be made subject to and in accordance with the provisions of these Regulations for the inclusion of that land in the appropriate register and for the registration of rights of common thereover and of persons claiming to be the owners thereof. (2) Where any land is for the time being registered under the Act, no application shall be entertained for its registration under these Regulations, and, where any land is for the time being registered under section 4 of the Act (whether or not the registration has become final) no application shall be entertained for the registration of rights of common over it."*

The procedure for the registration of New Land Regulation 3 land pursuant to s.13(b) of the 1965 Act remains for non-pioneer areas in terms of registration of new common land. No new town or village green may be registered under s.13(b), except *where such land is provided on an exchange in substitution for other land which is taken.* An application under New Land Regulation 3 for the registration of any substituted land may be made by any person.

Section 4

The effect is that s.13 by omission, and reg.3 by express provision, prevented the registration of any rights exercisable over land which was already registered under s.4 of the 1965 Act, i.e. land which fell within the initial registration procedure (hereafter referred to as "section 4 land"). Any grant of rights of common over land not registered under the 1965 Act s.4

procedure (mandatory initial registration) makes both land and rights eligible for registration under the provisions in ss.1 and 13 of the 1965 Act but a grant made before 2 January 1970 which was capable of being, but not, registered under s.4 of the 1965 Act before that date will is unexercisable and incapable of registration under s.13(b).

It had been suggested that no new rights of common may be registered over section 4 land by virtue of New Land Regulation, such rights nonetheless may be acquired over section 4 land (whether by grant or prescription). The consequence of these provisions is that there is the acquisition of new rights of common over existing registered common land—an express grant of a right of common—there would have resulted in an unregistrable and unexercisable right. The acquisition of a right of common by prescription over land not registered as section 4 land will make both the land and right eligible for registration.

But, in *Littlejohns*, the Court of Appeal held that a new right of common cannot be acquired by prescription over land registered under the 1965 Act. On the face of it, it concluded that new rights cannot be registered over New Land Regulation 3 land. This is because the Court of Appeal concluded that s.1(2)(b) of the 1965 Act renders unexercisable any right acquired over land already registered as common land. Moreover, the Court found that s.1(2)(b) of the 1965 Act, which renders unregistered rights unexercisable, has effect only in relation to rights exercisable over registered common land. This means that where a right is granted over unregistered land, it appears that there is no obligation to register either land or right. Rights granted over land which is not section 4 land (nor New Land Regulation 3 land) has the effect of creating new common land with both rights and land registrable pursuant to s.13(b) of the 1965 Act and under the provisions in New Land Regulation.

A grant of a right of common (or any sole right which is capable of being a statutory right of common) over any land which is not section 4 land, would cause that land to become common land, and to fall within the provision contained in s.1 of the 1965 Act that: *"there shall be registered any land which is common land"*.

Deregistration

An application for deregistration of the taken land may be made by a person who would have been entitled to apply under s.4 of the 1965 Act to claim ownership of the land. Such an application is made under General Regulation 27 for deregistration of the taken land.

Where an order is made by the Secretary of State for the deregistration, or deregistration and exchange, of land under s.17 of the 2006 Act, no application is necessary to enable the registers to be updated. Instead, the order acts directly against the registration authority, requiring it to update the registers in accordance with the order. In relation to non-pioneer registration areas, the order is to be treated as directing the registration authority to amend the registers which it maintains under the 1965 Act.

CHAPTER FOUR

HIGHWAYS AND MANORIAL WASTE

Often seen in Commons Land matters and commonly misunderstood. Back to basics.

Highways and Manorial Waste

Highways

One such example of the confusion caused by the 1965 Act is in relation to highways. The 1965 Act provided that common land meant "*land subject to rights of common…[or] waste land of a manor not subject to rights of common.*"

The 1965 Act also provides that, for the purposes of registration, *"'common land'…does not include…any land which forms part of a highway."*

'Highway' is not defined in the 1965 Act, but the term invariably means any way over which there is a public right to pass on foot, with or without a right of way for cycles, horses or vehicles. It follows that no land comprised in a highway qualified for registration under the 1965 Act.

The exclusion of highway land from registration under the 1965 Act was inserted because the then Ministry of Transport foresaw that land could be registered common land and highway, see Commons Registration Bill, notes on clauses, clause 20(2).

The exclusion did not seem to take into account unsurfaced highways (such as public footpaths and bridleways) across common land, which may have been unidentifiable on the ground, but were still technically required to be excluded from registration. It also did not appear to take into account, like averred here, the many highway verges, often of uncertain highway status, which were sometimes included in applications to register common land because they were also considered to be waste land of a manor.

Commons registration authorities responded in varying ways:

a. the authority registered the whole of the land identified in the application plan as common land, including any highway land;

b. the authority excluded any public roads from the land registered as common land;

c. the authority excluded all highways (including public rights of way) from the land registered as common land.

The result, therefore, is that the practice varies between commons registration authorities. In some authorities, the highways department of the authority objected to any registration of public roads (but rarely, it seems, to registration of public rights of way), and such objections were given effect by the commons registration department. In some cases, there was uncertainty about the status of land as highway verge and the highway department maintained an objection before the Commons Commissioners, who made a final decision.

This means that the register of common land reflects these different practices. For example, the registers for Dartmoor in Devon include public roads across the moor; the registers in Surrey invariably exclude public roads.

The 1965 Act, and the regulations made under it, are silent on the mechanism for giving effect to this exclusion. If it was intended that a registration authority should refuse to register any highway land, the legislation provided no machinery for it to do so, nor for an applicant to challenge an exclusion where the status as highway was in dispute. While there may be no doubt about the status of a classified road across a common, there might well have been difficulties in identifying the true width of the road, whether the highway included extensive verges, let alone the status of the many tracks and paths across common land which might or might not have been highways, and of uncertain width.

Where highway land has been excluded from registration under the 1965 Act, it cannot be assumed that the land is not subject to rights of common, because it is not registerable. If that is right, then s.1(2) of the Act cannot have had effect. Those advising ought to proceed on a common law basis that the 1965 Act had no application.

To the extent that manorial waste forms part of the highway, no registration under the Commons Registration Act 1965 is required. If it is not part of the highway, it must be registered under the Commons Registration Act 1965.

The highway may not extend to the physical boundaries. Adjacent land that does lie within the highway limits is given a name by the Highways Act 1980, section 130: *'roadside waste comprised in a highway'.* The words of section 130 concede that uncultivated land which lies open to a public road can be called roadside waste even when it is not comprised in the highway.

Manorial Waste

This has been described in *Attorney General v Hanmer* (1858) 27 L.J. Ch. 837.as:

> *"The true meaning of 'wastes,' or 'waste lands,' or 'waste grounds of the manor,' is the open, uncultivated and unoccupied lands parcel of the manor, or open lands parcel of the manor other than the demesne lands of the manor."*

This means that the 'waste' is:

a. open

b. uncultivated

c. uncopied

d. parcel of the manor.

Parcel of the manor has been understood to mean:

a. land which has its historical origin in the waste of the manor or,

b. the necessity of the land to continue to remain in the ownership of the lord of a manor.

In 1978 the Court of Appeal decided, in *Re Box Hill Common Box Parish Council v Lacy* [1977] B. No. 3702, that 'waste land of a manor' must still be in the ownership of the lord of the manor at the time the validity of the provisional registration was decided. This caused the commons commissioners to cancel many applications for registration of wastes which were not subject to rights, and which were no longer owned by the lord of the manor.

In *Hampshire CC v Milburn* [1991] A.C. 325 the case of *Box Hill* was overruled and it was stated that the land remained manorial waste and continued to qualify for registration.

Sadly, this would not undo the provisional registrations that had been cancelled since *Box Hill.* It did mean, however, that waste land could be registered as common land under the 1965 Act.

> *"The phrase 'waste land of a manor'... does not as a matter of legal language by any means necessarily import that the ownership of the land still rests with the lord of the relevant manor ... it is permissible to construe the phrase in this particular context of a post-1925 statute as meaning waste land which was once waste land of a manor in the days when copyhold tenure still existed..."*

For the purposes of registering the disputed waste land under and for the purposes of the Commons Registration Act 1965, therefore, it could be registered if at one time it was waste land of the manor, save that the time has lapsed to do so. Nevertheless, the Commons Act 2006 affords another chance for some wastes in England to be added back onto the register, where it can be shown that the land is manorial in origin even if it has long-since ceased to be owned by the lord of the manor. The Commons Act 2006 at s.4(2) will apply only if the land, *inter alia,* was provisionally registered as common land under s.4 of the Commons Registration Act 1965 but the registration was cancelled in certain circumstances.

Let's try and unpack *Hanmer.*

Reputed Manor

Sir Edward Coke (1552-1634) in his Institutes and Reports drew a distinction between true manors (a manor re et nominee) and reputed manors (a manor in nominee tantum). A reputed manor, was what a true manor became when land sales had reduced the number of free tenants to one, so that a court baron could not be held. In Crown Estate Commissioners, Lewison J observed that "most manors today" are reputed manors.

This is significant because before 1 January 1882, the conveyance of a reputed manor did not pass freehold interest of the grantor in the waste, or in any specific tenement possessed by the grantor unless there were express words to that effect – see *Doe D Clayton v Williams* (1843). The same applies to the transmission by Will, see Scriven on Copyholds (1896), p.5. The reason for particularity was to alleviate any doubt in respect of potential severance having operated prior to such transfer, and which arose as a result of the prohibition of subinfeudation.

If, therefore, a lordship title devolved where the manor ceased to be a true manor, the waste and specific tenements within the manor would not pass unless expressly conveyed.

However, section 62(3) of the Law of Property Act 1925 ('LPA 1925') states that the conveyance of a manor (for a reputed manor) includes "*all pastures, feedings, wastes, warrens, commons, mines...whatsoever to the manor appertaining or reputed to appertain, or at the time of the conveyance demised, occupied and enjoyed with the same, or reputed or known as part, parcel or member thereof*". In other words, you do not need to expressly convey the waste land. This assumes, however, that pre-commencement of the LPA 1925, a piece of land was still part of the manor.

Open

Open means unenclosed.

Inclosure of waste is an unequivocal act possible to indicate an intention that it should cease to be waste.

If land, formerly waste, has been enclosed it may be that its status as demesne consequent upon such enclosure can then be lost as a result of abandonment.

In *Re Rush Green, Harleston, Suffolk* [1979] 234/D/84, the Commissioner went on to consider whether demesne could revert to waste. His provisional opinion was that it could not and, in the absence of authority he expected to see evidence of abandonment of demesne status.

Uncultivated and unoccupied

This means land taken into arable cultivation or forestry is sufficient.

The purpose must be not merely temporary. For example conserving vegetation or tending to the wildlife constitutes a purpose that is greater than merely being on the land.

What courts look for is whether there was/is so much not done that it has since ceased to be land that is uncultivated waste.

There have been a few cases over the years on what constitutes uncultivated and occupied. They are not entirely consistent with each other. Take *Re Great Arden Moor,* for example. The question was whether the owner is using the land by taking in the sheep of other people to graze on it. The court decided that it was immaterial that the owners of the sheep are also tenants of other land belonging to the same owner. The use of land is sufficient to make it occupied and to take it out of the category of 'waste lands'.

In *Re Britford Common*, on the other hand, the Court did not find that land had ceased to be waste where the lord of the manor was "*taking its produce and cutting the grass for hay or silage*". The lord also could not be said to take the land "*simply by virtue of the lord of the manor taking its natural produce and in the absence of any inclosure of such land by the lord, which seems to me the vital point.*" The Court noted that:

> *"even when commoners had rights over waste land of a manor, the lord still had the right to every benefit to be derived from the soil of such land, provided only that he did not exercise it in a manner inconsistent with the rights of the commoners".*

Re Twm Barlwm Common went further, though, and found that:

> *"the fact that [the land] has been let is a relevant consideration but is not conclusive. A tenancy merely gives a right to occupy. If a tenant never goes to the land he has taken it may well remain unoccupied. If he does make use of it the question whether the land is 'occupied' is a question of fact."*

Practically speaking, one has a better chance of satisfying the test if there are improvements to the land sufficient to show an intention of exclusive and profitable use. Grazing is a use, for instance, but this is not necessarily enough to show occupation. If there is improvement to the land such as erecting a feeder, enclosing it etc, then this will constitute occupation. In many ways, the test is not dissimilar to factual possession in adverse possession cases.

CHAPTER FIVE

REGISTRATION: THE COMMONS ACT 2006

Understand the differences when it comes to registration and correction of the register in relation to different areas of England and Wales.

Common land must not be developed or encroached upon without the consent of the Secretary of State for Environment, Food and Rural Affairs (in England), or the Welsh Ministers, under section 38 of the 2006 Act, or without exchange land being provided under section 16 of the 2006 Act. What is hoped to be achieved by the 2006 Act, therefore, is a transparent and complete register so that members of the public and adjacent landowners know whether a right to walk (or ride) on the land can be exercised, or whether it can be developed.

Schedule 2 to Part 1 of the 2006 Act sets out what is intended to be a correction of the mistakes made under the 1965 Act.

Part 1 of Schedule 6 to the 2006 Act repeals the 1965 Act and sets out the maintenance and updating of the registers of common land and town or village greens. Part I of the Act, however, has not fully been brought into force. It only applies in nine pioneer areas of England.

The nine pioneer areas in England are:

a. Blackburn with Darwen

b. Cornwall

c. Devon

d. Herefordshire

e. Hertfordshire

f. Kent

g. Lancashire

h. Cumbria

i. North Yorkshire

Whilst there is a new UK government at the time of writing, there is still no timetable for transition.

For those that fall within the Pioneer areas, you can apply to register land as common land or town or village green where the land was omitted from registration under the 1965 Act, but is identified as common land, or green, in or under a statute.

If the land is designated under a scheme of management and regulation made under Part I of the Commons Act 1899, is subject to a deed conferring access under section 193(2) of the Law of Property Act 1925, or was excepted from registration under section 11(1)–(4) of the 1965 Act, then there is hope that it will be registered under the 2006 Act.

The 2014 regulations and guidance, for the pioneer areas, and the 2017 regulations for Wales and guidance, prescribe the process for making applications to amend the registers of common land and town and village greens.

Correcting mistakes and de-registration

Schedule 2 to Part 1 of the 2006 Act sets out how and what can be corrected. Section 22 of the 2006 Act gives effect to Schedule 2. This makes provision for rectification of certain mistakes, omissions and other matters in the registers prepared under the 1965 Act.

Section 19 of part 1 of the 2006 Act sets out how to correct the registers of common land or town or village greens. If and when land becomes registered under the 2006 Act, it will be included in accessible maps as per the Countryside and Rights of Way Act 2000.

An application for any of the purposes contained in Schedule 2 to the 2006 Act (see below) may be made only on a prescribed form. It can be made by any person, but must be made before the prescribed cut-off date:

a. 31 December 2020: in relation to the authorities pioneering implementation of Pt 1 from 2008;

b. 15 March 2027: in relation to the second tranche authorities pioneering implementation of Pt 1 from 2014;

c. 15 March 2027—in relation to the non-pioneer registration authorities; (

d. 4 May 2032—in relation to Wales.

This means that at the end of December 2020, the period allowed for making applications under schedule 2 in the pioneer areas came to an end. This means applications under schedule 2 can no longer be made in these areas.

Applications to the common's registration authorities of Cumbria and North Yorkshire, respectively to correct mistakes in these areas under schedule 2, paragraphs 2, 3, and 5, on the other hand, is still capable of being made. It must be made on or before 15 March 2027.

Elsewhere in England, applications can be made but only to deregister land under paragraphs 6, 7, 8 or 9 of schedule 2. Applications under these provisions must be made by 15 March 2027.

Paragraphs 2 to 9 of schedule 2 set out when a mistake or non-registration can be rectified:

a. Paragraphs 2 and 3: apply to land that was designated as common land or village green by or under an Act of Parliament but not registered under the 1965 Act;

b. Paragraph 4: applies to land that was provisionally registered as common land under the 1965 Act but the registration was cancelled in certain circumstances;

c. Paragraph 5: applies to land that was registered as common land but ought to have been registered as a town or village green;

d. Paragraph 6: enables the deregistration of common land that has been covered by a building or its curtilage since provisional registration. This is intended to capture common land that may have been mistakenly registered so as to include houses or gardens on, or abutting, the common. The position must have existed at the time of the original provisional registration, and thereafter at all times up to the date of determination of the application or proposal. If the building has been demolished in the intervening period, provided that it was immediately replaced, then the test is still satisfied as being throughout the period;

e. Paragraph 7: enables the deregistration of certain other land that was wrongly registered as common land. his provision is not restricted to buildings and curtilage (as it is under para.6). But land can be considered under this paragraph only if it was provisionally registered as common land under s.4 of the 1965 Act, its provisional registration was not referred to a Commons Commissioner, and the land then became finally registered. An application or proposal cannot be made where a hearing was originally held into the registration of the land by the Commons Commissioner. In *Re West Anstey Common* [1985] Ch. 329, the Court of Appeal held that, on a referral to the Commissioner, the registration of the whole of the land comprised in the registration was considered. There was an inquiry under s.6 of the 1965 Act at which the Commissioner ought to have heard objections from a landowner to a provisional registration. If, however, the disgruntled landowner did have the opportunity to object, then s.7 prevents a renewed attempt to seek deregistration. An application or proposal under this paragraph will succeed if one can show that, before provisional registration, the land was not:

   i. subject to rights of common;

   ii. manorial waste land;

   iii. a town or village green as per the 1965 Act; or

   iv. land subject to be inclosed under s.11 of the Inclosure Act 1845.

b. Paragraph 8: enables the deregistration of a town or village green that has been covered by a building since provisional registration. Sub-paragraph (3) provides that the latter element of the criterion is satisfied if, and only if:

i. Due to its physical nature, the land was unusable by members of the public for pastimes throughout the period of 20 years before its provisional registration under the 1965 Act; and

ii. immediately before its provisional registration the land was not and at the time of the application is still not allotted by or under any enactment for the exercise or recreation of the inhabitants of any locality.

c. Paragraph 9: the deregistration of certain land wrongly registered as a town or village green. It must be shown that:

i. the land was (immediately before provisional registration) not common land subject to rights of common and not manorial waste;

ii. the land was, during the period of 20 years prior to provisional registration, physically unusable for pastimes, and

iii. the land was (immediately before provisional registration) not allotted for recreation.

The Commons Registration (England) Regulations 2014 – applications – North Yorkshire and Cumbria (paras 2, 3 and 4)

When applying to rectify a mistake under Schedule 2, the application must include:

a. evidence of how paras 2, 3 (with evidence of consent of the owner) or 5 are satisfied.

   If the land in question is covered by a building or which is within the curtilage of a building it may be registered under para 3 only if the owner of that land consents to its registration;

b. a copy of any order, local acts or enactment, if there is any. This includes any award and any consent required by the owner of a building or curtilage of a building;

c. a map at a scale of at least 1:2,500 (save in moorland areas, where a scale of at least 1:10,560 applies) showing the application land.

If the land was provisionally registered as common land under the 1965 Act but was cancelled in certain circumstances, then paragraph 4 of Schedule 2 applies and one can apply to re-register. This applies to land that was provisionally registered as common land under section 4 of the 1965 Act i.e. between 1967 and 1970 and there was an objection to its provisional registration, and one of the following applies:

a. para 4(3): the registration was cancelled by the commons commissioner because the land had ceased to be connected with the manor;

b. para 4(4): the registration was cancelled by the commons commissioner because the land was not subject to rights of common, and the commissioner did not consider whether it was waste land of the manor. This was designed to remedy the fall out after *Box Hill* until overruled in *Minburn* years later;

c. para 4(5): the registration was cancelled at the request of or with the agreement of the applicant before or after referral to a commons commissioner. The reasoning for including this lies in the suggestion that registration of the land is a matter of

public interest, and that, had a commoner not caused the land to be registered as

common land with initial provisional registration of a right of common exercisable over it, another person (having no legal interest in the common) might have chosen to do so.

An application can be made if the land is 'waste land of a manor' at the date of application (see earlier chapter). The deadline for applications is 15 March 2027.

Paragraphs 6, 7 8 or 9 of Schedule 2 (elsewhere in England, and North Yorkshire and Cumbria, that is not a pioneer authority area)

Anyone can apply (it is not necessary that the applicant is the owner or tenant of the land). The application must include:

a. evidence of how the criteria (in para 6, 7, 8 or 9) are satisfied;

b. a fee: determined by the registration authority;

c. a map at a scale of at least 1:2,500 (save in moorland areas) showing the application land.

Practical considerations

If applying to register or deregister land under any provision in schedule 2 one will be required to show in the application details of the provisional registration of the land under the 1965 Act. To find this out, look at the commons registers and records held by the registration authority.

To make an enquiry, the following will be needed:

a. contact details;

b. the name of the parish or district;

c. name or location of the common or village green;

d. the rights entry number

A fee is payable for an application under any of paragraphs 6 to 9 of Schedule 2. There is no fee for applications under paragraphs 2 to 4. If a fee is paid under paragraphs 6 to 9, and the application is referred to the Planning Inspectorate, a further fee is payable.

Include maps i.e it must be an Ordnance Survey map, with a scale of at least 1:2,500 to show any land you to be added or removed from the register, unless the land is wholly or predominately moorland in which case an Ordnance Survey map with a scale of at least 1:10,560 is sufficient.

However, if you are applying to register land under paragraphs 2 to 5 of schedule 2 to the 2006 Act, and the area included is the entirety of a cancelled register unit, the register unit may be referenced.

The application will be advertised by the registration authority upon the application being filed.

The registration authority must also serve a notice of the application by email on anyone who has previously asked to be informed of all applications and proposals. Notice must also be served on persons specified in Schedule 7 to the 2014 Regulations, including, in all cases, any person who has declared an entitlement to exercise a right of common, any person who is registered as the owner of a right of common held in gross, and any commons council.

If referred to the Planning Inspectorate, a hearing may be held.

Section 19

Section 19 applies in England and Wales. This is for limited purposes and there is no time-limit for applications. This allows applications to be made for the rectification of the registers to correct a mistake made by the commons registration authority when making or amending an entry in the register of common land or register of greens (section19(2)(a)).

An application can may be made in the following circumstances only in the areas of pioneer authorities and 2014 authorities in relation to:

a. correcting mistakes not affecting the extent of the land or quantification of rights, i.e. any other mistake (section 19(2)(b));

b. removing a duplicate entry (section 19(2)(c));

c. updating the name and address in an entry (section 19(2)(d));

d. updating to take account of accretion or diluvion (section 19(2)(e)).

Anyone can apply under section 19 providing the application is made on the prescribed form and includes:

a. a statement of purpose i.e. the purpose for which the application is made under section 19(2);

b. details of the register unit if known;

c. evidence of the mistake;

d. the intended correction;

e. a map at a scale of at least 1:2,500 (save in moorland areas) showing the application land;

f. payment of fees, where applicable, for section 19(2)(b), (d) and (e). None is payable where there is a wider public interest as in sections 19(2)(a) or (c).

Where the mistake was made by the registration authority this is not limited to pioneer areas and 2014 authorities.

The authority may not correct a mistake under section 19 if it considers that by reason of reliance reasonably placed on the register by any person, or for any other reason, it would in all the circumstances be unfair to do so S.13(3) of the 2006 Act) This "fairness" test mirrors s.14 of the 1965 Act. This enabled the court to order rectification of the register in certain circumstances where "the court deems it just to rectify the register."

The Supreme Court considered "fairness" in *Betterment Properties (Weymouth) Ltd v Dorset County Council (No.2); Paddico (267) Ltd v Adamson* [2014] UKSC 7. It has ruled that developers' delays in challenging the initial registration of land as a town or village green under s.14(b) of the 1965 Act, were not, in the particular facts of the cases, prejudicial to any party and should be permitted. Reference was made to the doctrine of laches, and that a lapse of time between the registration and an application to rectify under s.14 might constitute a bar to relief where (a) there was knowledge of the facts, and (b) acquiescence, or (c) detriment or prejudice.

A prejudice may include where a commoner has relied on a right of common as registered under the 1965 Act and then proceeded to operate a farm holding at a price and had no reason to doubt it. Applying what is fair and considering that the prejudice caused would be to remove what the commoner has built/operated on the land over years, a Court is more likely to refuse an alteration to the register, even if the provisional registration was incorrect in the first place because of an error made by the registration authority.

Proposal to amend by the Registration Authority

A registration authority may itself make a proposal for amending the register for the same purposes for which an application can be made under section 19, paras 2 to 9 of Schedule 2, or para 2 of Schedule 3.

Before taking any other steps in relation to a proposal to amend the register, a registration authority must prepare a statement in writing describing the proposal and explaining the justification for it.

The registration authority may not proceed with a proposal under Schedule 2 to the 2006 Act unless it has complied with this requirement, and with the duty to publicise a proposal, on or before 31 December 2020, in relation to the original pioneer authorities, and 15 March 2027, in relation to the second tranche pioneer authorities.

It must also display a notice of the proposal on site and serve a notice of the proposal on the following:

a. the owner of any part of the land comprised in the register unit to which the proposal relates;

b. any person who has made a declaration, duly recorded in the register, of entitlement to exercise a right of common over any land comprising the whole or any part of the register unit to which the proposal relates;

c. any commons council, or other body;

d. any owner of a right of common in gross which is exercisable over any part of the land comprised in the register unit to which the proposal relates. In relation to both applications and proposals, notice need not be served on the owners of rights of common held in gross where they are too many to make service reasonably practicable; and

e. every other local authority for the area (including a parish council).

There is no provision in the 2006 Act for a registration authority to make a proposal for any other purpose, even where the authority is the owner of that land.

Appeals

The High Court may order the register to be amended if information in an entry or the entry itself has been secured by fraud and it would be just to amend it, s.19(7) of the 2006 Act.

Under the 2006 Act, there is no statutory appeal like s.14(b) of the 1965 Act. Section 14 of the 1965 Act remains in force in relation to the non-pioneer registration areas.

An application may be made to seek leave for judicial review of a registration authority.

CHAPTER SIX

USE AND DEVELOPMENT OF COMMON LAND

Registration as common land affects the use and development of the land.

Registers can be inspected in person, or a non-statutory search can be carried out as part of the conveyancing process using form CON 29O.

Vehicular Access

Restrictions have been set out in legislation. Pursuant to section 193 of the Law of Property Act 1925 ('LPA 1925') driving a carriage, cart, caravan, truck or other vehicle over an urban or metropolitan common, or a common to which the section has been applied by deed under subsection (2) of section 193 is an offence, unless the person has "lawful authority" i.e an authority given by an owner of a common. This does not mean the owner of a common can allow a driver to commit a nuisance or commit a criminal offence.

It is also an offence to drive a mechanically propelled vehicle on to or upon any common land without lawful authority under s.34(1) of the Road Traffic Act 1988, unless the land is within 15 yards of a road and used only for parking.

Can there be a right to drive a vehicle over a common by prescription under the Prescription Act 1832 or pursuant to the doctrine of lost modern grant?

Bakewell Management Ltd v Brandwood [2004] UKHL 14 put this to bed. When the common land was sold to Bakewell, an injunction and declaration was granted against the surrounding land owners to prevent them from using the land, who then appealed. The Court was asked to decide whether the illegal use of the land (crossing the land with vehicles contrary to the LPA 1925) prevented the acquisition of a right of way or whether there was a presumption of a lost modern grant. Given permission for access over the land with vehicles had never been consented to, the Court found that a lost modern grant could not be presumed where an actual grant by a landowner would have been unlawful. However, there was no requirement of public policy that prevented an easement from being established where the grant would remove the criminality of trespass by creating a right to access. The case of *Hanning v Top Deck Travel Group Ltd* (1994) 68 P. & C.R. 14 was held to be wrong in law on the grounds that an easement over land can be lawfully granted by the landowner or established by long-user or prescription whether the use relied on is illegal (criminally) or tortiously. This does not mean to say an easement by prescription can be obtained if neither the owner nor any other person has the dispensing power to trigger a presumed grant.

Sustainable Farming Incentive Agreement ('SFI')

An SFI pays you for actions that can help reduce farm input costs, reduce waste, improve soil health and help mitigate the impacts of extreme weather. The Rural Payments Agency has opened applications for the expanded SFI offer from summer 2024 in a controlled way, so everyone gets the right level of service and support.

For the purposes of an SFI agreement, 'common land' means:

a. land registered as common land in a register of common land kept under Part 1 of the 2006 Act;

b. land to which Part 1 of the 2006 Act does not apply and which is subject to rights of common within the meaning of the 2006 Act.

'Shared grazing' means communal pasture that is not registered as common land where graziers have a legal entitlement to graze. For example, a pasture used jointly by tenants.

To enter common land into an SFI agreement, you must:

a. meet the Basic Payment Scheme (BPS) (now replaced with the interlinked scheme) eligibility requirement for common land (eligible for BPS in2021, 2022 or 2023);

b. be a single entity, either as a sole beneficiary or a group:

    i. Before applying for an SFI agreement, a group must take reasonable steps to contact and consult everyone with a legal interest in managing the common land. This is to make sure they:

        a. are aware of the group's intention to enter the common land into an SFI agreement

        b. have the chance to participate in the SFI agreement

        c. The people with a legal interest in managing the common land include:

            i. all known common rights holders, whether they're actively using their rights or not

            ii. the landowner

iii. tenants

iv. anyone who has an easement or other rights and covenants over the land, including sporting tenants

c. have a formal, legally enforceable internal arrangement for a group;

d. have sufficient management control of the common land to complete the SFI actions for the duration of the 3-year SFI agreement:

   i. The land type must be eligible for the SFI actions you choose at the start of your SFI agreement;

   ii. What SFI action you do will depend on the type and feature. The DEFRA Guidance: SFI actions you can do on different eligible land types and features, updated 6 June 2024, sets out these actions according to land type in tablature form;

   iii. There is also the Summary of initial expanded SFI offer from summer 2024 which has other actions included;

   iv. Each action has a code and this is what is referenced in the SFI form;

   v. This does not mean that every commoner has to agree or become part of the single entity. However, it does mean that those who are part of the single entity need to be able to complete the SFI actions in the SFI agreement for the single entity to have sufficient management control of the land;

vi. Those with management control tend to mean:

   a. an owner occupier who's either farming or managing the land themselves or employing a contractor;

   b. a tenant with a Farm Business Tenancy ('FBT') under the Agricultural Tenancies Act 1995, or an Agricultural Holdings Act 1986 tenancy; or

   c. group farming or managing common land (including areas of shared grazing).

An SFI agreement on common land operates in the same way as an SFI agreement on land outside a common. If the SFI agreement conflicts with any statutory requirements for the management of the common, those statutory requirements take precedence. For example, if the common land is a site of special scientific interest.

Your SFI agreement's total annual payment value is based on:

a. what you have entered into your selected SFI actions – in hectares, metres, square metres (for traditional buildings) or the number of features (such as ponds);

b. the additional payment per agreement if you have entered land into actions such as under code CSAM1 or CMOR1;

c. SFI actions you have selected that apply to an SFI agreement, rather than a specific area of land such as code CIPM1;

d. the year of your agreement;

e. any additional common land payment for group agreements. To help with the costs of administering an SFI agreement on common land, there is an annual additional payment of £7 per hectare of eligible common land entered into its own SFI agreement.

Towards the end of each agreement year, you must submit an annual declaration to confirm you have complied.

Delinked Payments

The Rural Payments Agency (RPA) replaced the Basic Payment Scheme (BPS) in England with delinked payments in 2024.

The BPS was a payment for farmers who carried out eligible agricultural activities. The farmer or crofter must have been actively farming the land. In England, entitlements were allocated to farmers in respect of registered common land on the basis of "right of use", as opposed to actual use.

To qualify, commoners must have been "using" the common such as:

a. exercising a right of common by turning out stock on the common;

b. participating in an agri-environment agreement in respect of the common; or

c. contributing to managing the common.

The BPS has been replaced from 1 January 2024 with delinked payments. To qualify you must:

a. be eligible – this means you must have claimed, and been eligible for, BPS payments in England in the 2023 scheme year (or inherited eligible land after 15 May 2023);

b. have a reference amount.

The value of your payments for 2024 to 2027 will not be affected if:

a. your farm size changes

b. you change what the land is used for, after BPS 2022 (the last year of the reference period).

The reference amount will be the average of the BPS payments for 2020, 2021 and 2022.

Fencing against a common

There is a general duty in common law to fence so as to contain animals. This stems back to the 1400s.

As to their own livestock, it is the duty of the commoner to contain the commoner's livestock and is broadly the same as it is for any other grazier.

As to the duty to fence against a common, this has been considered in the Courts, as has the status of customary laws. In *Crow v Wood* [1971] 1 Q.B. 77 the Court concluded that a customary origin for the obligation to fence against a common could not exist. Instead, the Court considered the operation of easements. In *Churston Golf Club Ltd v Haddock* [2019] EWCA Civ 544, the Court of Appeal considered itself bound by *Crow v Wood* and did not seek to review it despite the latter case of *Egerton v Harding* [1975] Q.B. 6 suggesting otherwise. In *Egerton v Harding* [1975] Q.B. 6 the court decided that there was a customary duty to fence land against cattle straying from the waste land class of common land and as such a duty to fence against a waste land type of common can lie in custom; there is no need to consider easements.

Another case concerning custom was *New Windsor Corporation v Mellor* [1974] 1 WLR 1504 where a local authority was prevented from building on land because the local people proved that there was a custom that they had the right to use the land for lawful sports.

As to the standard of fencing, in *Coaker v Wilcocks* [1911] 2 K.B. 124 the Court concluded that a Dartmoor farmer was not expected to hedge against non-traditional high-jumping Scottish sheep. The standard of fencing required is only that necessary to keep out the local breed and be reasonably secure.

Where a custom to fence against a waste can be established but an animal escapes, the Courts have considered to what extent knowledge of dilapidation plays a part. In the event of an escape, the onus of proof lies on the commoner to establish that there has been a breach of a duty to fence. In *Sutcliffe v Holmes* [1947] K.B. 147 the claimant averred that damaged had been caused by straying sheep. The Defendant said a third party was in default of its duty to fence against the common. The Court concluded that the wrongful act of a third party provided a defence in cattle trespass. This means, however, that when deciding this, the Court has to consider whether the defendant knew or ought to have known of the defective fences, and ought to have taken steps to have the defects remedied.

If the fencing is in disrepair, a commoner, properly in possession of a right of common, can bring an action for damages or a mandatory injunction to compel repair.

Development of common land

Pursuant to section 38 of the 2006 Act, a person may not, except with the consent of the Secretary of State,1carry out "restricted works" on registered common land and certain other land which is recognised as common land.

Consent may be given under s.38(1) of the 2006 Act:

a. in relation to all or part of the proposed works; and

b. subject to such modifications and conditions relating to the proposed works as the Secretary of State thinks fit.

To see what conditions might be attached see *Common land guidance sheet 6: Section 38 consent dealing with modifications and conditions*, Planning Inspectorate (January 2015).

Restricted works means preventing or impeding access to or over the land, together with works for the resurfacing of land. Residents, as well as councils, have brought proceedings over the years to prevent restricted works from being carried out. For example, in *Eaton v Kurton*, a commoner brought a claim and asserted that a hardcore track across the common, intended to provide access to a property, was a "*construction of any other work*". HHJ Rawlings found:

> *"the construction of that way had impeded or was likely to impede access to the land by the very nature of the way itself. Even more. in my view, it is clear that the presence of traffic upon the way would, in circumstances to be envisaged, impede the passage of cattle or other animals entitled to graze upon the land."*

If what is being done, however, is customary, such as erecting fences, it is doubtful this would be regarded as restricted works requiring consent.

Defra has said that:

> *"... works take place on common land only where they maintain or improve the condition of the common or where they confer some wider public benefit and are either temporary in duration or have no significant or lasting impact."*

Section 39(1) of the 2006 Act sets out the criteria to which the Secretary of State must have regard when assessing an application:

a. the interests of persons having rights in relation to, or occupying, the land (and in particular persons exercising rights of common over it);

b. the interests of the neighbourhood;

a. the public interest (in nature conservation, conservation of landscape, the protection of public rights of access and the protection of archaeological remains and features of historic interest); and

b. any other matter considered to be relevant.

Examples of restricted works to which when consent may be granted to further this vision include lambing sheds, car park barriers, works for the purposes of generating renewable energy, new gates and stiles, seating, dredging, supports or netting for loose rocks, etc. Consent is likely to be granted if the works are inextricably linked to how the land is being managed and used. A refusal of consent may be challenged in the courts. The decision whether to grant consent is by the Planning Inspectorate.

The procedure for making an application is regulated by the Works on Common Land etc. (Procedure) (England) Regulations 2007.

After completing the application (the pro forma being referenced in the regulations), and after a period of advertisement, if not dealt with on paper and an inquiry is to be held, the inspector may hold a pre-inquiry meeting to determine the matters to be addressed and the procedure to be followed at the inquiry.

An environmental impact assessment ('EIA') may be (and is often advised to be) required to assess the likely significant environmental effects of the proposed works.

Consent may be sought by way of a retrospective application. But for works which have been completed without consent, there is a risk of enforcement under s.41 of the 2006 Act before any application is approved or if an application is refused.

On an application under s.41, the court may order the removal of works lacking consent it can adjourn proceedings to allow an application to be made retrospectively, grant the order or, or make compliance with any order for reinstatement conditional on the application being refused.

An action under s.41 of the 2006 Act is subject to the 12-year limitation period in s.8 of the Limitation Act 1980, running from the date on which the unlawful works were erected, because it is said that an action would fall within the meaning of a "specialty", see *Collin v Duke of Westminster* [1985] Q.B. 581.

Where there is an interference with commoners' rights under common law, they are entitled to the peaceful enjoyment of their rights of common. Where the rights of a commoner are interfered with, the remedy is an action for damages or a claim for an injunction or both.

Under s.45, any "ownerless" common may be protected by the local authority. The authority may take all necessary steps to protect it as if it were the owner in possession.

CHAPTER SEVEN

WHAT IS A VILLAGE GREEN?

(Written by Penny Emmott)

This chapter describes what a village green is,

Village greens are a patch of land in a village used by its inhabitants for recreational use. In *R v Oxfordshire CC Ex p. Sunningwell Parish Council [20002] A.C. 335* Lord Hoffman fondly referred to a village green *"with its memories of maypole dancing, cricket and warm beer."*

Immemorial Customary Right

The essential legal characteristic of a green is that the inhabitants have an immemorial customary right to use it. There is no legal difference between a village green and a town green, it simply depends in which type of settlement it is situated.

An immemorial customary right is one that is proven to have existed in 1189, in other words, the beginning of legal memory. The position is summarised in *Megarry & Wade: The Law of Real Property (Sweet & Maxwell, 10th ed, 2024), paragraph 26-050* as follows:

> *"A custom really amounts to a special local law, a local variation of the common law. The common law recognises such variations only if they are ancient, certain, reasonable and continuous. To be "ancient" a custom must date back to the year 1189, the beginning of legal memory; but ancient*

> *origin may be presumed if there has been long enjoyment and there is no proof of a later origin."*

To establish a custom as far back as 1189 posed obvious evidential difficulties and as a result, the law in recognising immemorial customary rights over greens has developed on the basis of a series of presumptions, all of which are rebuttable by evidence to the contrary;

1) First, the courts presumed that an act had occurred conferring lawful title upon the person in possession or enjoyment of the customary right to use the green before 1189.

2) Second, that in the absence of direct evidence, the existence of the customary right in 1189 could be presumed on the basis of evidence of long-term use of the right.

3) Third, that the period of long-term use was presumed to be established upon evidence of the customary right for the period of "living memory".

4) Fourth, upon the introduction of a fixed 20-year time limit for possessory actions pursuant to the Limitation Act 1623, evidence of the customary right for a period of 20 years raised the presumption that it had existed in 1189.

This final presumption is reflected in the current regulatory regime at section 15 of the Commons Act 2006 which requires all new town and village greens to be registered. The core requirement is that *"a significant number of the inhabitants of any locality, or of any neighbourhood within a locality, have indulged as of right in lawful sports and pastimes on the land for a period of at least 20 years"* (s15(3)(a)).

This has allowed the courts to establish immemorial customary rights where it could not have previously such as in the case of *Fitch v Rawling (1795) 2 H. Bl. 393; 126 E.R. 614* where Buller J recognised a custom to play cricket as having existed since 1189 despite the game not being in existence at the time.

Examples of the courts recognising customary rights include:

a. For the holding of a fair or wake *(Wyld v Silver [1963] Ch. 243);*

b. For inhabitants to *"enter upon certain land in the parish, and erect a maypole thereon, and dance round and about it, and otherwise enjoy on the land any lawful and innocent recreation at any times of the year" Hall v Nottingham (1875) 1 Ex. D. 1.*

The case of *New Windsor Corp v Mellor [1975] 3 W.L.R. 25* sets out that once established, a customary right cannot be lost by either disuse or abandonment. It can similarly not be lost if the custom itself has changed over time.

The Inclosure Act 1845

Legislation has recognised the significance of the village green since the Inclosure Act 1845 which required Inclosure Commissioners to consider allocating land between four and ten acres for exercise and recreation when making an inclosure award.

This practice was adopted largely because of the growing public concern of the time that large scale urbanisation would put an end to the protection of open spaces.

Land could therefore become a green by either establishing an immemorial customary right or by allotment in an inclosure award under the Inclosure Act 1845.

The Commons Registration Act 1965

A Royal Commission on Common Land 1958 (1958) Cmnd 462 recommended that *"as the last reserve of uncommitted land in England and Wales, common land ought to be preserved in the public interest."*

As a result, the Commons Registration Act 1965 was enacted, establishing a register of common land and greens and recording rights of common. The definition of a town or village green is set out at section 22:

> *"In this Act, unless the context otherwise requires... "town or village green" means land which has been allotted by or under any Act for the exercise or recreation of the inhabitants of any locality or on which the inhabitants of any locality have a customary right to indulge in lawful sports and pastimes or on which the inhabitants of any locality have indulged in such sports and pastimes as of right for not less than 20 years."*

Under this Act registration of town and village greens was required which were to be classified in three ways as established by case law including *R v Suffolk CC Ex P. Steed [1995] Q.B. 487* and *R v Oxfordshire CC Ex p. Sunningwell PC [2000] 1 A.C. 335.*

The position is summarised in *Megarry & Wade: The Law of Real Property (Sweet & Maxwell, 10th ed, 2024), paragraph 26-051:*

1. Class A: land which has been allotted by or under any Act for the exercise or recreation of the inhabitants of any locality;

2. Class B: land on which the inhabitants of any locality have a customary right ot indulge in lawful sports and pastimes; and

3. Class C: land on which for not less than 20 years a significant number of inhabitants of any locality, or any neighbourhood

> (or neighbourhoods) within a locality, have indulged in lawful sports and pastimes as of right, and either continue to do so or have ceased to do so for not more than such period as may be prescribed or determined in accordance with prescribed provisions.

Under the 1965 regulatory scheme, applications to register common land, greens and rights of common were invited between 2nd January 1967 and 2 January 1970, they were provisionally granted unless and until anyone made an objection to their registration until 31st July 1970.

The effect of not registering a green that was capable of registration was confirmed in *Oxfordshire CC v Oxford City Council [2006] 2 A.C. 674* where Lord Hoffman found that the effect of non-registration was:

> *"to extinguish such rights of recreation as may have existed by custom or statutory allotment and were registrable on the appointed day."*

The Commons Registration Act 2000

A lot of the 1965 Act has been repealed by the Commons Registration Act 2000 including the definition of town or village green. Under s98 of the 2000 Act it was defined as:

> *"...land which has been allotted by or under any Act for the exercise or recreation of the inhabitants of any locality or on which the inhabitants of any locality have a customary right to indulge in lawful sports and pastimes as of right for not less than twenty years or which falls within subsection (1A) of this section.*

1A Land falls within this subsection if it is land on which for not less than 20 years a significant number of inhabitants of any locality, or of any neighbourhood within a locality, have indulged in lawful sports and pastimes as of right, and either;

(a) Continue to do so, or

(b) Have ceased to do so for not more than such period as may be prescribed or determined in accordance with prescribed provisions."

This change in definition (1) removed the need for use by people from the locality itself (2) introduced "any neighbourhood within a locality" and (3) introduced a power for the Secretary of State to make regulations to establish the period where qualifying use has ceased – no such regulations have been introduced.

The Commons Act 2006

The aim of the Commons Act 2006 is to improve and modernise the law on registration and protection of common land and town and village greens. When in force, the CA 2006 will repeal the whole of the CRA 1965. However the provisions are being brought into force over time.

Section 15 of the CA 2006 permits applications to register new village and town greens where *"a significant number of the inhabitants of any locality, or of any neighbourhood within a locality, indulged as of right in lawful sprots and pastimes on the land for a period of at least 20 years."* This section is one of the few sections of the CA 2006 that is fully in force across England.

The introduction of the Growth and Infrastructure Act 2013 has introduced further restrictions on the registration of new greens under s15 of the CA 2006 which will be explored in more detail in the next chapter.

CHAPTER EIGHT

REGISTRATION AND MANAGEMENT OF A VILLAGE GREEN

Basics you should know about registration and what one has to prove to register a Green.

Registration

Land that qualifies is land which has been used for at least 20 years for sports and pastimes by a significant number of inhabitants. Where 20 years' recreational use as of right has accrued, a landowner who then gives permission for the use will not prevent the use being as of right. Subject to the extent, acts like construction, substantial landscaping, installing Connection Media, etc, may constitute a substantial interruption. Whether it is temporary will be a matter of fact and degree (physical extent and duration).

The Land may include water and if only a part of it has been used as set out aforesaid, the registration may apply to the whole parcel of land having regard to the physical condition of the land during the relevant period. All that matters is that it satisfies the test hereinafter and common sense must prevail, see *R (on the application of Cheltenham Builders) v South Gloucestershire Council* [2003] EWHC 2803 (Admin).

A neighbourhood is not a sub-division of a locality, and need not be a recognised administrative unit. What one must look for is natural defining features such as a road, local facilities nearby and whether there is a community feel. There is no definition in the Commons Act 2006 and those reading are advised to look at the definition in other statutory regimes such as *R (on the application of Cheltenham Builders) v South Gloucestershire Council* [2003] EWHC 2803 (Admin). Neighbourhood is not singular, see *Leeds Group v Leeds CC* [2010] EWHC 810 (Ch).

As to what is a sport and pastime, it was stated in *R v Oxfordshire CC Ex p. Sunningwell Parish Council* [2000] 1 A.C. 335 that:

> *"sports and pastimes' is not two classes of activities but a single composite class which uses two words in order to avoid arguments over whether an activity is a sport or pastime"*

In *R v Oxfordshire CC Ex p. Sunningwell Parish Council* [2000] 1 A.C. 335 Lord Hoffman confirmed that there may be cases where the user is *"trivial or sporadic so as to not carry the outward appearance of user as of right"*. It is important to distinguish use to determine whether a reasonable landowner would understand there is the exercise of lawful sports and pastimes across the whole land. This is also important when determining whether the use is akin to the exercise of a right of way or not. As is said by Lord Hoffman in *R. v Oxfordshire CC Ex p. Sunningwell Parish Council* [2000] 1 A.C. 335:

> *"But walking a dog, jogging or pushing a pram on a defined track which is situated on or traverses the potential Green may be recreational use of land as a Green and part of the total such recreational use, if the use in all the circumstances is such as to suggest to a reasonable landowner the exercise of a right to indulge in lawful sports and pastimes across the whole of his land. [...] The critical question must be how the matter would have appeared to a reasonable landowner observing the user made of his land, and in particular whether the user of*

> *tracks would have appeared to be referable to use as a public footpath, user for recreational activities or both. [...]"*

As it was put by Lord Carnwath in *R (on the application of Barkas) v North Yorkshire CC* [2014] UKSC 31; [2015] A.C. 195:

> *"the conduct must bring home to the owner, not merely that 'a right' is being asserted, but that it is a village green right".*

Confirmation has been given by the Supreme Court in *R (on the application of Lewis) v Redcar & Cleveland BC* [2010] 2 A.C. 70 that "as of right" under section 15 of the Commons Act 2006 is *"sufficiently described by the tripartite test nec vi, nec clam, nec precario"* in the context of prescriptive acquisition of rights of way.

There is no express power in the Commons Act 2006 and 2014 regulations to register a smaller area of land than that applied for. In *Oxfordshire CC v Oxford City Council & Robinson* [2004] Ch. 253; [2006] Ch. 43 (CA); [2006] 2 A.C. 674 (HL) the Court confirmed that a registration authority is entitled, without any amendment of the application, to register only that part of the application land which the applicant/s has proved to have been used for the necessary period.

Section 15(1) of the Commons Act 2006 provides that any person may apply to a registration authority to register land as a town or village green, where one of subsections (2), (3) or (4):

> *"...a significant number of the inhabitants of any locality, or of any neighbourhood within a locality, have indulged as of right in lawful sports and pastimes on the land for a period of at least 20 years."*

This is largely the same as s.22(1A) of the Commons Registration Act 1965.

Where access has been prevented because of statutory prohibitions such as foot and mouth outbreaks, bird flu and Covid-19, those periods are disregarded when determining the 20 years period, see section 15(6) of the Commons Act 2006.

The Common Act 2006 confirmed the conditions for the registration of new greens. It made important changes to how and in what circumstances those conditions could be met. Until registered, the land is not a Green and to qualify:

a. The use continues at the time of the application; or

b. The use ceased before the time of the application but after the commencement of section 15, and the application is made within a period of one year after use has ceased; or

c. the use ceased before the commencement of section 15, and the application is made within a period of five years after the cessation of use, s.15(4) (the latest being April 2022).

The 20 years may be interrupted and have to restart if the landowner makes a declaration to negate the registrability of the land as a Green, see section 15A(1) of the Commons Act 2006. If this happens, local communities have a period of grace. If a declaration is made, a map identifying the land in the prescribed form must be included.

The prescribed requirements are in the Commons (Registration of Town or Village Greens) and Dedicated Highways (Landowner Statements and Declarations) (England) Regulations 2013 (as amended) including:

a. the above mentioned map;

b. regulation 2 compliant statement;

c. publicity by way of notice in the form set out in Schedule 2 and posted for not less than 60 days on the land, on the boundary and/or online.

Such notices are more effective for landowners to protect against future registration than attempting to prevent access to land.

Where 20 years use as of right for lawful sports and pastimes has accrued prior to the deposit of a landowner statement under section 15A of the Commons Act 2006, the deposit triggers the period of grace under section 15(3).

If land is acquired compulsorily and is to be used for a defined statutory purpose, the public cannot acquire by use rights that are incompatible with it. This was confirmed in *R (on the application of Newhaven Port and Properties Ltd) v East Sussex CC* [2015] UKSC 7; [2015] A.C. 1547.

This is not to be confused with trigger events. Section 15C excludes the right to apply to register land as a new green when a particular event in planning under the town and country planning system has occurred in relation to the land. Under section 15C(2), when a trigger event has occurred, the right to apply under becomes exercisable again when a terminating event (such as a proposal no longer being live by planning having been revoked or expired) occurs in relation to the land. Such events are set out in Schedule 1A of the Commons Act 2006. This includes trigger events that predate the commencement of the Commons Act 2006.

Where potential development land is at risk of being subject to a village green application, a land developer may avoid undertaking pre-application consultation because it put the local inhabitants on notice. The land identified for potential development was interpreted in *R (on the application of Cooper Estates) v Wiltshire Council* [2019] EWCA

Civ 840 wherein the Court accepted that the land subject to the village green application could be part of a larger area of land identified for potential development in a plan.

It is open to landowners to also apply to register land as a Green under s.15(8). This is often to avoid development post compulsory purchase.

To register a new Green, and subject to whether the disputed land is in a pioneer area, the 2014 Regulations SI 2014/3038 apply. The regulations set out certain requirements at Regulation 16 and Schedule 4 paragraph 9:

a. OS Map;

b. Evidence that section 15 of the Commons Act 2006 is satisfied in respect of the application land;

c. Description of the application land; and

d. Description of the locality or the neighbourhood relied upon.

Whilst under regulation 20(2) the registration authority may ask for more information it is best to not leave it to chance and include all information as per the regulations. Thereafter it must be publicly advertised for at least 42 days. Any objection must be received in that time.

Acquisition and Disposal

Land which is registered as a village green can be bought and sold.

The value of the Green, however, will be influenced by rights of local inhabitants to use the land for recreation. This may result in the reduction of use by the landowner.

Valuation was considered in *Betterment Properties v Dorset CC & Taylor* [2010] EWHC 3045 (Ch) wherein the Court observed that the operation of the Commons Registration Act 1965 was such that land can be a town or village green in law even if the land is unattractive with little amenity value. The amenity value to local residents, however, may lie in them being able to continue walking their dogs or walking on said land. The Court looked at *hope value* i.e the value of the land in the event that registration is cancelled and, for example, planning permission could be obtained or the land otherwise be used for agricultural purposes. In that case a valuer looked at what the value was, as at the date of purchase, when the land was subject to registration as a green but there was a prospect of that registration being removed by rectification, (hope value), where the hope was that rectification would be ordered and the hope value was in between the lower value where the land was registered as a green and the higher value where the land was not registered as a green. The Court concluded that Betterment can show that it will be at a substantial disadvantage by reason of the registration as compared with the case where the land was not registered as a green:

> *"That difference is represented by a substantial amount in money terms. When Betterment bought the land, it paid more than the land was worth if the land were to remain registered as a green; it paid less than the value of the land if the registration were to be rectified. That is precisely what one would expect with a purchase of land where its value is subject to uncertainty as to a future event"*

For those reading that act for those contemplating purchasing land which is registered, do not assume that the register may be rectified or registration cancelled. A judge will find your client to have proceeded with their eyes open, knowing of the risk. In *Betterment,* it was only because the Court concluded on the facts of that case that continuation of a registration that ought not to have been made in the first instance, and will cause substantial harm to any landowner, that rectification of the register was ordered. Registration as a green is likely in most cases to prevent any proposed development or intensive agricultural use of the land.

To determine if the land sought to be purchased is a village green, enquiries can be made of local authorities on the purchase of land, known as CON 29O, and of the commons registration section of the local authority. It is suggested that this be done as well as enquiries made of the seller.

Exchange and De-Registration

As alluded to above, a Green can cease to be registered. Pursuant to section 16(1) of the Commons Act 2006, the owner can apply for the land to cease to be registered.

Land up to 200 square metres may be released from registration but any land greater than that will require a proposal for replacement land to be registered in lieu of the released land. Public interest, the interests of those in the land and the interest of the neighbourhood are all relevant factors. Applications are often refused if there is no such replacement land available and/or there is no replacement land of equal to the land proposed to be released. Public consultation prior to the application is advised.

The application may be referred to the Planning Inspectorate in certain circumstances such as if the registration authority has an interest in the outcome. Confidence in the decision might be undermined if left with the registration authority to decide.

The Commons (Registration of Town or Village Greens) (Interim Arrangements) (England) Regulations 2007 apply at the time of writing to all commons registration areas save for the pioneer areas in which the 2014 Regulations apply.

Applications must be made in accordance with the 2007 Regulations and in particular comply with the following requirements:

a. made on Form 44;

b. signed by every applicant who is an individual, and by the secretary or some other duly authorised officer of every applicant which is a body corporate or unincorporate;

c. provision of a copy every document relied on;

d. supported:

    i. by a statutory declaration as set out in Form 44;

    ii. further evidence as, at any time before finally disposing of the application, the registration authority may reasonably require.

Objections may be made and the decision lies with the registration authority.

Use and Extent

As confirmed in *R (on the application of Lewis) v Redcar & Cleveland BC* [2010] 2 A.C. 70, you will not find the register will say, nor will the answers to enquiries necessarily say, that the nature and extent of any right/use exercise on the land is e.g shooting, sports etc. Once registered as a green, land can be used generally for sports and pastimes even if the original sport was, for example, shooting that justified registration of the land as a green in the first instance.

However, where the landowner's previous use of the land during the relevant 20-year period prevented some lawful sports and pastimes from occurring, they could not occur after registration. This does not mean a landowner is excluded from the land as a result of registration. The landowner is able to use the land in any way which does not interfere with the recreational rights of the local inhabitants. As was said in *Lewis* the rights of the landowner and the local inhabitants could coexist with "*give and take*" on both sides. Inhabitants have to use the land in a lawful manner and not unlawfully, unfairly or improperly exercise their recreational rights because to do so means they go beyond the established custom and become trespassers, see *Fitch v Fitch* (1797) 2 Esp. 543; 170 E.R. 449.

Equally, if the agricultural use of the land after registration changes and prevents or otherwise significantly interferes with the recreational use which local inhabitants had been able to make of the land prior to registration, that goes beyond an allowable use. This does not mean that intermittent grazing, for instance, cannot take place. Providing what he landowner is doing is not incompatible the actions/use are not unlawful.

As to land which already had a pre-existing recreational use during the relevant 20-year period whilst qualifying use was also made of the land by local inhabitants, that pre-existing use should be able to continue unaffected.

The "*relevant inhabitant*" captures inhabitants of the relevant locality or neighbourhood in relation to which the land was registered. This means that if a non-local inhabitant were to use the Green, a landowner may prevent them from doing so, see *Buckinghamshire Mental Health NHS Foundation Trust) v Oxfordshire CC* [2010] EWHC 530 (Admin).

Unhelpfully, under the 1965 Act, there was no requirement to register the locality having use or the benefit of the registered Green. For the Pioneer Areas, the 2014 Regulations SI 2014/3038 require that an application to register land as a Green under section 15(1) of the 2006 Act "*contain a description of the locality or the neighbourhood within a locality relied upon*", see also paragraph 9(c) of Schedule 4 of the 2014 Regulations.

As per Regulation 3(2) of the Commons (Registration of Town or Village Greens) (Interim Arrangements) (England) Regulations 2007) an application is made using Form 44 and this allows the registrant to state the locality. Regrettably, this is not repeated in the register.

The practical effect, or at least for none of the pioneer areas, is that a landowner will be unable to stop a person/s from using the Green because it is unknown to whom it is intended to benefit and for what specific purpose.

Open Spaces Act 1906

A local authority and local council groups/organisations can manage and control an open space acquired under or dedicated to the purposes of the Open Spaces Act 1906 to further public recreation via bye laws.

Commons Act 1899

A district council may vest the management of land in the council that is registered as a Green.

Nuisance and Occupiers Liability Acts

Section 29 of the Commons Act 1876 concerns public nuisance and makes it a criminal offence to:

a. Encroach on or enclose a Green;

b. Erect on a Green, save where to do so is to improve the Green such as a band stand.

Installation of necessary Connection Media would not fall within 'Nuisance'.

Only works allowed on a Green that are done with a view to the better enjoyment of the Green, or do not injure the land or interrupt the use or enjoyment of the land as a place for exercise or recreation will be acceptable.

Those that can bring proceedings include:

a. A local authority (s.222 of the Local Government Act 1972);

b. Member of the public or private individual if special damage suffered.

The remedy sought will often be an injunction but for nuisance, those affected may seek to abate for themselves.

The grant of an easement by the landowner and beneficiaries of the same would fall in the above category because there can be no rights of common acquired by prescription. This does not mean that a landowner cannot continue a pre-existing use – this is not a public nuisance.

Section 12 of the Inclosure Act 1857 protects greens from nuisance by creating a criminal offence of wilfully causing a nuisance. This means the commission of any act which injures the land or which interrupts the use or enjoyment of the land as a place for exercise or recreation. What the Court would look for is:

a. whether there has been material harm to the green or an interference with the public's recreational enjoyment;

b. the extent of the green affected;

c. duration of the interference.

If works needed to the land are more than betterment and/or do injure the land, deregistration or an exchange of land will be necessary under sections 16 and 17 of the 2006 Act, to allow works to be undertaken on the Green. This does not mean that a landowner has to do works of maintenance to the better enjoyment of the Green such as fencing.

A landowner or occupier with sufficient degree of control over the land, however, has a duty to use care to prevent injury to a person on the land. The Occupiers' Liability Act 1957 applies to lawful visitors and the Occupiers' Liability Act 1984 applies to persons who are trespassers. Whilst there is no requirement as a landowner to do works of maintenance to the better enjoyment of the Green, the landowner owes a duty, as the occupier, to ensure the land is safe. As *Gautret v Egerton* (1867) L.R. 2 C.P. 371 confirms, the granting of the use by the landowner may be regarded as a gift. This means that the way, for example, need not be put into a better state of repair/security as it was when permission to use it was first granted.

More generally, a landowner may otherwise be liable for injury on the Land if they are:

a. aware of the danger or has reasonable grounds to believe that it exists;

b. know or have reasonable grounds to believe that the trespasser is in the vicinity of danger;

c. the risk is one the landowner in all the circumstances may be expected to reasonably offer protection.

If there is a right conferred by law, such as the right of inhabitants to use a Green for sports, they are treated as visitors under the Occupiers' Liability Act 1957.

Other criminal offence

Pursuant to the Road Traffic Act 1988, section 34, it is an offence to drive a vehicle onto a Green without lawful authority. By vehicle this mans a "mechanically propelled vehicle". Where this leaves the CPS or private prosecutions where what is used is an e-scooter or-bike, for example, where it is not strictly mechanically propelled, remains to be seen.

MORE BOOKS BY LAW BRIEF PUBLISHING

A selection of our other titles available now:-

'A Practical Guide to Probation Breaches and Other Applications' by Mark Thomas
'A Practical Guide to Remarriage and Divorce' by Cordelia Williams & Claire Howard
'A Practical Guide to Privacy, Transparency, Reporting Restrictions and Closed Proceedings in the Court of Protection' by Laura Mannering
'Beaumont on Barristers – A Guide to Defending Disciplinary Proceedings (Second Edition)' by Marc Beaumont
'A Practical Guide to Payments for Environmental Services' by Ben Sharples
'A Practical Guide to the Law of Pregnancy and Maternity at Work' by Rebecca Thomas
'A Practical Guide to Redundancy – Second Edition' by Philip Hyland & Collette Moore
'A Practical Guide to International Issues for Scottish Family Lawyers' by Susie Mountain, Donna McKay, Ken MacDonald
'A Practical Guide to the Law on Deprivation of Liberty' by Ben Troke
'A Practical Guide to Rights over Airspace and Subsoil – Second Edition' by Daniel Gatty
'A Practical Guide to the Law in Relation to Inquests' by Ramya Nagesh
'A Practical Guide to the Construction and Rectification of Wills and Trust Instruments (Second Edition)' by Edward Hewitt
'A Practical Guide to Data Protection in Social Housing' by Clare Paterson
'A Practical Guide to Spousal Maintenance – Second Edition' by Liz Cowell
'A Practical Guide to International Parental Child Abduction Law (England and Wales)' by Dr Onyója Momoh
'A Practical Guide to Deprivation of British Citizenship' by Sean Ell
'A Practical Guide to Commercial Property Service Charges' by Rachel Garton
'A Practical Guide to Clinical Negligence – Third Edition' by Geoffrey Simpson-Scott (Geoff)
'A Practical Guide to the Rights of Grandparents in Children Proceedings – Second Edition' by Stuart Barlow

‘The Electronic Communications Code: A Practical Guide – Second Edition’ by Kerry Bretherton KC, James Castle, Mark Loveday

‘A Practical Guide to the Independent School Standards – September 2023 Edition’ by Sarah McKimm

'A Practical Guide to Estate Administration and Crypto Assets' by Richard Marshall

‘A Practical Guide to Parental Alienation in Private and Public Law Children Cases’ by Sam King QC & Frankie Shama

‘Contested Heritage – Removing Art from Land and Historic Buildings’ by Richard Harwood QC, Catherine Dobson, David Sawtell

‘The Limits of Separate Legal Personality: When Those Running a Company Can Be Held Personally Liable for Losses Caused to Third Parties Outside of the Company’ by Dr Mike Wilkinson

‘A Practical Guide to Transgender Law’ by Robin Moira White & Nicola Newbegin

‘A Practical Guide to ‘Stranded Spouses’ in Family Law’ by Mani Singh Basi

‘A Practical Guide to Residential Freehold Conveyancing’ by Lorraine Richardson

‘A Practical Guide to Pensions on Divorce for Lawyers’ by Bryan Scant

‘A Practical Guide to Challenging Sham Marriage Allegations in Immigration Law’ by Priya Solanki

‘A Practical Guide to Digital Communications Evidence in Criminal Law’ by Sam Willis

‘A Practical Guide to Legal Rights in Scotland’ by Sarah-Jane Macdonald

‘A Practical Guide to New Build Conveyancing’ by Paul Sams & Rebecca East

‘A Practical Guide to Inherited Wealth on Divorce’ by Hayley Trim

‘A Practical Guide to Practice Direction 12J and Domestic Abuse in Private Law Children Proceedings’ by Rebecca Cross & Malvika Jaganmohan

‘A Practical Guide to Confiscation and Restraint’ by Narita Bahra QC, John Carl Townsend, David Winch

‘A Practical Guide to the Law of Forests in Scotland’ by Philip Buchan

‘A Practical Guide to Health and Medical Cases in Immigration Law’ by Rebecca Chapman & Miranda Butler

‘A Practical Guide to Bad Character Evidence for Criminal Practitioners by Aparna Rao

‘A Practical Guide to Extradition Law post-Brexit’ by Myles Grandison et al

‘A Practical Guide to Hoarding and Mental Health for Housing Lawyers’ by Rachel Coyle

'Stephens on Contractual Indemnities' by Richard Stephens
'A Practical Guide to the EU Succession Regulation' by Richard Frimston
'A Practical Guide to Solicitor and Client Costs – Second Edition' by Robin Dunne
'Constructive Dismissal – Practice Pointers and Principles' by Benjimin Burgher
'A Practical Guide to Religion and Belief Discrimination Claims in the Workplace' by Kashif Ali
'A Practical Guide to the Law of Medical Treatment Decisions' by Ben Troke
'Fundamental Dishonesty and QOCS in Personal Injury Proceedings: Law and Practice' by Jake Rowley
'A Practical Guide to the Law in Relation to School Exclusions' by Charlotte Hadfield & Alice de Coverley
'A Practical Guide to Divorce for the Silver Separators' by Karin Walker
'The Right to be Forgotten – The Law and Practical Issues' by Melissa Stock
'A Practical Guide to Planning Law and Rights of Way in National Parks, the Broads and AONBs' by James Maurici QC, James Neill et al
'A Practical Guide to Election Law' by Tom Tabori
'A Practical Guide to the Law in Relation to Surrogacy' by Andrew Powell
'A Practical Guide to Claims Arising from Fatal Accidents – Second Edition' by James Patience
'A Practical Guide to Asbestos Claims' by Jonathan Owen & Gareth McAloon
'A Practical Guide to Stamp Duty Land Tax in England and Northern Ireland' by Suzanne O'Hara
'A Practical Guide to the Law of Farming Partnerships' by Philip Whitcomb
'A Practical Guide to the Law of Unlawful Eviction and Harassment – Second Edition' by Stephanie Lovegrove
'A Practical Guide to Costs in Personal Injury Claims – Second Edition' by Matthew Hoe
'A Practical Guide to the General Data Protection Regulation (GDPR) – Second Edition' by Keith Markham
'A Practical Guide to Working with Litigants in Person and McKenzie Friends in Family Cases' by Stuart Barlow
'Protecting Unregistered Brands: A Practical Guide to the Law of Passing Off' by Lorna Brazell
'A Practical Guide to Secondary Liability and Joint Enterprise Post-Jogee' by Joanne Cecil & James Mehigan

'A Practical Guide to the Pre-Action RTA Claims Protocol for Personal Injury Lawyers' by Antonia Ford

'A Practical Guide to Neighbour Disputes and the Law' by Alexander Walsh

'A Practical Guide to Coercive Control for Legal Practitioners and Victims' by Rachel Horman

'A Practical Guide to the Law of Driverless Cars – Second Edition'

by Alex Glassbrook, Emma Northey & Scarlett Milligan

'A Practical Guide to TOLATA Claims' by Greg Williams

'A Practical Guide to Elderly Law – Second Edition' by Justin Patten

'A Practical Guide to Responding to Housing Disrepair and Unfitness Claims' by Iain Wightwick

'A Practical Guide to the Law of Bullying and Harassment in the Workplace' by Philip Hyland

'How to Be a Freelance Solicitor: A Practical Guide to the SRA-Regulated Freelance Solicitor Model' by Paul Bennett

'A Practical Guide to Prison Injury Claims' by Malcolm Johnson

'A Practical Guide to Advising Clients at the Police Station' by Colin Stephen McKeown-Beaumont

'A Practical Guide to Antisocial Behaviour Injunctions – Second Edition' by Iain Wightwick

'Practical Mediation: A Guide for Mediators, Advocates, Advisers, Lawyers, and Students in Civil, Commercial, Business, Property, Workplace, and Employment Cases' by Jonathan Dingle with John Sephton

'The Mini-Pupillage Workbook' by David Boyle

'A Practical Guide to Crofting Law' by Brian Inkster

'A Practical Guide to the Law of Domain Names and Cybersquatting' by Andrew Clemson

'A Practical Guide to the Law of Gender Pay Gap Reporting' by Harini Iyengar

'NHS Whistleblowing and the Law' by Joseph England

'Employment Law and the Gig Economy' by Nigel Mackay & Annie Powell

'A Practical Guide to Noise Induced Hearing Loss (NIHL) Claims' by Andrew Mckie, Ian Skeate, Gareth McAloon

'An Introduction to Beauty Negligence Claims – A Practical Guide for the Personal Injury Practitioner' by Greg Almond

'Intercompany Agreements for Transfer Pricing Compliance' by Paul Sutton

'Zen and the Art of Mediation' by Martin Plowman

'A Practical Guide to Adoption for Family Lawyers' by Graham Pegg

'A Practical Guide to Industrial Disease Claims' by Andrew Mckie & Ian Skeate
'A Practical Guide to Conducting a Sheriff Court Proof' by Andrew Stevenson
'A Practical Guide to Vicarious Liability' by Mariel Irvine
'A Practical Guide to Applications for Landlord's Consent and Variation of Leases' by Mark Shelton
'A Practical Guide to Relief from Sanctions Post-Mitchell and Denton' by Peter Causton
'A Practical Guide to Equity Release for Advisors' by Paul Sams
'A Practical Guide to Financial Services Claims' by Chris Hegarty
'A Practical Guide to Financial Ombudsman Service Claims' by Adam Temple & Robert Scrivenor
'A Practical Guide to Running Housing Disrepair and Cavity Wall Claims – Second Edition' by Andrew Mckie & Ian Skeate
'A Practical Guide to Holiday Sickness Claims – Second Edition' by Andrew Mckie & Ian Skeate
'Arguments and Tactics for Personal Injury and Clinical Negligence Claims' by Dorian Williams
'A Practical Guide to Drone Law' by Rufus Ballaster, Andrew Firman, Eleanor Clot
'On Experts: CPR35 for Lawyers and Experts' by David Boyle
'An Introduction to Personal Injury Law' by David Boyle

These books and more are available to order online direct from the publisher at www.lawbriefpublishing.com, where you can also read free sample chapters. For any queries, call us on 0844 587 2383 or email us at mail@lawbriefpublishing.com.

Our books are all generally in stock at www.amazon.co.uk with free next day delivery for Prime members, and at good legal bookshops such as Wildy & Sons.

We are regularly launching new books in our series of practical day-to-day practitioners' guides. Visit our website and join our free newsletter to be kept informed and to receive special offers, free chapters, etc.

You can also follow us on Twitter at www.twitter.com/lawbriefpub.

www.ingramcontent.com/pod-product-compliance
Lightning Source LLC
LaVergne TN
LVHW022112200926
848481LV00003B/1144
9781914608414